Why National Parks?

Ian O. Brodie

Written by Ian O. Brodie

ISBN 978-1-904098-52-2

Published by:
Wildtrack Publishing,
Venture House,
103 Arundel Street,
Sheffield S1 2NT

Typeset and processed by Christine Handley

Front cover photograph: © Ian O. Brodie

CONTENTS

Foreword v

Preface vi

Acknowledgements vi

Introduction 1

Chapter 1: The Vision for National Parks 11

Chapter 2: The National Park Vision - access for walkers 53

Chapter 3: The Landscape Vision for National Parks 79

Chapter 4: Whither National Parks? 97

Bibliography and Sources 133

FIGURES

Cover: Hart Crag, Deepdale in the Lake District National Park

1. John Dower
2. Malham Cove, Yorkshire Dales National Park.
3. Dower's Map 1 of his suggested first ten National Parks in England, and Wales.
4. Dower's Map 2 Showing the 'Distribution of areas to be considered when National Parks in England and Wales are selected.'
5. Looking north from the Stiperstones, Shropshire Hills AONB.
6. Bury and Amberely Wildbrooks, South Downs National Park.
7. Near Hatchett Pond, New Forest National Park.
8. Ingram Brough Law to Cushat Law, Northumberland National Park.
9. Rev. H. H. Symonds
10. Dovedale, Peak District National Park.
11. Tom Stephenson.
12. Tarr Steps, Exmoor National Park.
13. Cader Idris, Snowdonia National Park.
14. Bonehill and Grimspound, Dartmoor National Park.
15. Pen-y-Fan and Cribin, Brecon Beacons National Park.
16. Stanton, Gloucestershire within the Cotswolds AONB.
17. The River Tees below Cronkley Scar, the North Pennines AONB. A potential National Park?
18. Ramsey Island, Pembrokeshire Coast National Park.
19. Staithes, North Yorkshire Moors National Park.
20. Warm Beck Gill, Roeburndale, Forest of Bowland AONB. An AONB with a greater proportion of access land than most National Parks.

The picture of John Dower is by kind permission of the Dower family; Tom Stephenson is reproduced by kind permission of the Ramblers' and that of H. H. Symonds by courtesy of Friends of the Lake District. All other pictures are copyright to the author.

Foreword by Lord Rooker

Why National Parks?

One thing is for sure - if the founders had not got the National Parks when they did, we not only would not have them today - we would not get them today.

The procrastination over the latest two in New Forest and South Downs shows what we would be up against. My recent evidence is from Northern Ireland when I proposed the first National Park and encountered massive opposition.

Dartmoor might be secure due to terrain and weather patterns, but the Peak and Lake District National Parks would be heavily fought against nowadays. "Vested interest old boy" I can hcar them saying. The Stalinist approach of many local councillors who hide behind the mantle of elections would oppose the loss of planning approvals to unelected bodies.

We all have a responsibility whether or not we use our National Parks to be considered guardians for the future.

The landscape belongs to us all even if the land belongs to someone.

Jeff Rooker
A walker.

Preface

National Parks and Areas of Outstanding Natural Beauty are, in statute, the highest forms of landscape protection in England and Wales. After sixty years they are perhaps more controversial than at any time in their history. This book looks at the visions of the two main proponents of National Parks, the landscape protection and access movements, and asks how far their post-war expectations have been met. The book asks if the current family of supporting organisations has succeeded or failed to explain their significance for the nation and, if we re-visit these early values, will the future of designated landscapes be more secure?

Acknowledgement

My thanks go to Andrew Dalby for making valuable suggestions to the manuscript and to Jeff Rooker for his foreword. The book also recognises the work of many campaigners for National Parks, many no longer with us, and without their unstinting efforts, our most significant landscape areas would not benefit from statutory protection.

INTRODUCTION

The British concept of designated landscapes is quite unique when compared with National Park designations elsewhere in the world. Nowhere, as in many parts of the world, in the British Isles do we have landscapes of such wildness nor do we have areas of land where we find a huge variety and intensity of wildlife living to the virtual exclusion of human interference.

The English, Welsh and, more recently, the Scottish, idea of landscape designations is drawn from a long history usually dated to Wordsworth's *Guide to the Lake District.* (Wordsworth, 1810). The concept developed through major conservation campaigns of which Thirlmere in the 1870s was paramount, and then was catalysed by the Great War, the depression of the 1930s and finally World War II. Such a period of gestation led to the designation of our National Parks and areas of outstanding natural beauty, which today are generally well recognised by the public even if never far from political skirmishes.

The history of this movement is not the subject of this publication. It has been well covered especially by Cherry (1975) and a host of well-informed commentators. Our current list of landscape designations as a product of the outcome of this history can be read as questioning their validity in the twenty-first century. Certainly if we started out with the landscape designation process today, we might find a totally different structure and administration for these precious areas. The history is vital to understanding where we are now and to answering the question as to the fitness for purpose of our National Parks and Areas of Outstanding Natural Beauty in the twenty-first century.

To consider fitness for purpose solely based on the knowledge of history and the current political movements would be insufficient and short-sighted for beneath the purpose of designation is a range of philosophies, values and attitudes which have rarely been actively considered and re-stated since prior to the Dower Report of 1945. [John Dower, pictured below] This book seeks to analyse the thinking, the values, the ethos that provided the rationale that led the pioneers of the National Park movement to campaign for such designations. Without understanding their hopes and the values on which they based their arguments any future debate on the merits of these areas would prove sterile and futile.

Figure 1: John Dower

Whilst the National Park movement was a national campaign across England and Wales, significantly its origins and many of its major proponents were based, or were active, in the North-West and particularly the Lake District. Recent publications by Cousins (2009) and Brodie (2012) underline the Lake District's significance. So whilst this book considers national matters it is appropriate to recognise that many roots of this national amenity campaign lie within the north-west.

One of several reasons the debate about the merits of our landscape designations is current is due to the potential extension of the boundaries of the Lake District and Yorkshire Dales National Parks. This throws the debate back firmly into our region and provides the opportunity to reiterate what has erroneously, for around seven decades, fallen off the agenda of almost all landscape campaigning and governmental bodies, the need to understand why we have these designations.

Prior to re-drawing a boundary for our designated areas or, perhaps of interest for the future, considering the designation of new areas there is an assumption that we understand why we designate landscapes as National Parks or as areas of outstanding natural beauty. This assumption of the visions for landscape protection and appropriate recreational use of what we regarded as our finest landscapes in 1951, in those years of post-world war hope, is that the underlying rationales are still as valid today. There is a mistaken assumption that we widely accept and understand why we need to protect some landscapes (and provide appropriate recreational access) in preference to other areas which can often be landscapes local communities value immensely. However, when, since 1951, have those of us who cherish our designated landscapes considered and articulated why such an approach is still valid some 60 years on? Why have we not felt the need to restate our visions for such areas during times of threats to the integrity of these areas? It can be argued the books of Marion Shoard (1987 & 1999) along with those of Ann & Malcolm MacEwen (1982 & 1987) tried to stimulate this debate. Phillips' recent paper (2010) shows there is within the National Park family an emerging need for the debate to be re-opened. This is written at a time when it is noted that staff within some National Park authorities are seriously questioning the relevance of the two statutory purposes of National Park designation. It is clearly appropriate to revisit the vision the founders of the movement inculcated into our statutory process. From the outset there was a recognition, that even if the designated landscape concept was more widely understood, there would be still many detractors. These have been recognised over decades as George Trevelyan notes:

'to speak more precisely, those of us who care for preservation of natural beauty are still out-numbered and overbourne by those who, though not all of them, wholly indifferent to our cause place other considerations whether of business or of politics in a higher place than any such considerations.' (Trevelyan, 1929)

The essence of the vision for National Parks was identified by Blenkinsopp as *'The National Parks stand for a scale of values that is in conflict with many of the pressures of our urban society.'*(Blenkinsopp, 1975) Therein lies the vision and the enigma we have to face today. So great can be the battles, as A. Wragg suggests, the continued attrition of landscape is unrelenting, it brings into question the protected areas approach of National Parks and of areas of outstanding natural beauty.(Wragg, 2000) Paul Shepheard describes our current British landscape strategy as *'the economic exploitation of the earth'* from which we *'are simultaneously rewarded and deprived.'*(Shepheard, 1997) If Wragg is correct then the strategy for their future needs consideration.

Rene Dubos notes another of the potential problems of designating cultural landscapes for preservation:

'On the one hand, we extol the virtue of the wilderness and want to preserve it intact for its own sake. ...We fight on their behalf because we believe in their right to existence and in

their importance as unique forms of creation. On the other hand, we resent any change in our environmental heritage, even though it was created out of wilderness by human activities.'

Dubos further reminds us that the landscapes we want to protect are already much changed from being entirely natural:

'We struggle to save these human creations, forgetting that all of them represent areas deforested, swamps drained, hillsides gouged of their stones and sand. In brief, we want to save both the wilderness and the environments that have been created by destroying the wilderness.' (Dubos, 1980)

Charges of wanting to "protect wilderness" are levelled at the conservation movement despite the conservation movement readily accepting, within Britain, Dubos' understanding of how the landscapes have evolved in human time.

The implementation and work of the National Park authorities and their vision has, since the 1949 Act according to Ann and Malcolm MacEwen, been going '*downhill (nearly) all the way.'* (MacEwen, 1982) Perhaps if we can rediscover an appropriateness to life today in the spirit of the founders' visions we may have the ability to re-promote the values of our National Parks and turn the onslaught of those who see them as barriers to their, often personal, economic interest. Perhaps now is the time for us to consider what are the purposes of National Parks and areas of outstanding natural beauty, and if and why we might, as a nation, still need these designations. Since the MacEwens produced their seminal work the staff of National Park authorities and AONBS have changed and the current staff of these bodies have not all had the benefit of a grounding in the ethos of the movement for which they work. In some cases, they are alleged to be questioning the very relevance to their work of the statutory purposes.

The significant questions include –Why has the National Park movement lost its wider public understanding and thus support? How valid today and for the future are the values that led to the designation of National Parks? Why should we discriminate in favour for only part of the countryside to be protected more strongly (if we actually do)? Is there a vision and rationale for the National Park movement to regroup and re-establish designated landscapes as a significant contribution to meet the needs and aspirations of present and future societies without compromising the viability of the original and vital values? Alternatively, has the case for designated areas been overtaken by the changing demands of modern society?

To me after some forty years personal involvement in the National Park movement, it appears strange that we are still now asking the question – what are National Parks and who and what are they for? How do we today help people to understand that some areas of our finest landscape need the highest levels of protection? In addition, how do we show that their protection is for the wider benefit of humanity?

In Chapter 1, I look at the context for the derivation of the values and purposes of designated landscape. Although the focus is on National Parks much of the narrative can be applied to Areas of Outstanding Natural Beauty. Chapter 2 examines the values established by the open air access movements whilst Chapter 3 looks at the values and ethos established by the landscape protection movement. Finally, I examine the relevance of these values today and ask if and why we still need these designations and, if so, what these values should be in the twenty-first century.

Being based in the Lake District and aware that the area was on most people's lists of potential National Parks at the time of Dower and Hobhouse, I may appear to give the examples in the book a bias towards this National Park. However, given the origins of the landscape preservation movement and the interest of many of the founder members of the National Park movement this is perhaps a good starting point to write this book.

Time Line

These are the major dates, especially for parliamentary processes, relevant to understanding the evolution of our thinking on designated areas. See also Cousins (2009), Hill (1980) and Darby (2000) for other significant events.

1810 Wordsworth's call for "a sort of national property."
1877 First mention of National Parks in a parliamentary debate.
1877-1879 The campaign against turning Thirlmere into a reservoir regarded as the birth of the landscape conservation movement.
1884/1888 First Bills brought before Parliament to seek to provide access to mountains.
1894 The National Trust Act.
1905 The formation of the Federation of Rambling Clubs.
1926 Formation of the Council for the Preservation of Rural England (CPRE now the Campaign to Protect Rural England).
1931 Addison Report on National Parks.
1932 The most famous "mass trespass" on Kinder Scout.
1935 Ramblers' Association formed.
1935 Standing Committee on National Parks set up (CNP now the Campaign for National Parks).
1942 Scott Report on Land Utilization in Rural Areas.
1945 Dower Report on National Parks.
1947 Hobhouse Report on National Parks.
1949 National Parks and Access to the Countryside Act.
1968 Countryside Act.
1981 Wildlife and Countryside Act.

1994 UK signs the Convention on Biological Diversity.
2000 Countryside and Rights of Way Act.
2006 Natural England and Rural Communities Act.
2007 British government signs the European Landscape Charter.
2013 Public inquiry into extensions to the Lake District and the Yorkshire Dales National Parks.

Governmental Bodies responsible for Designated Areas

1949 - 1968: National Parks Commission (NPC)
1968 - 1999: Countryside Commission (CC)
1999 - 2006: Countryside Agency (CA)
2006 - to date: Natural England (NE)

Figure 2: Malham Cove, Yorkshire Dales National Park

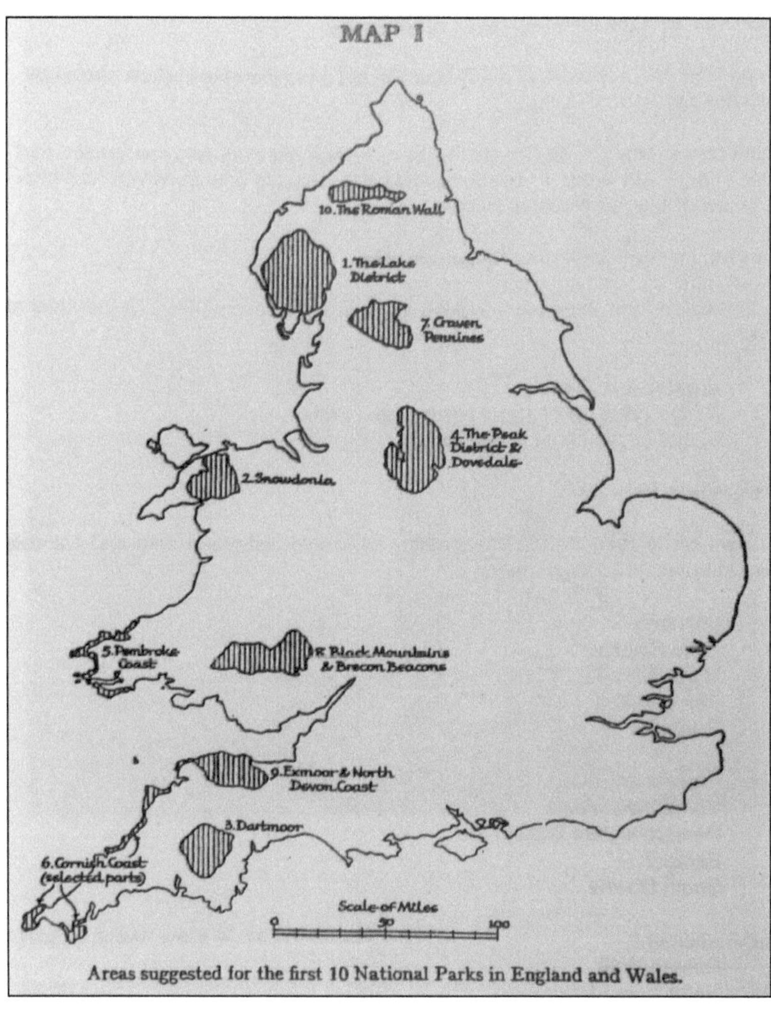

Areas suggested for the first 10 National Parks in England and Wales.

Figure 3: Dower's Map 1 of his suggested first ten National Parks in England and Wales

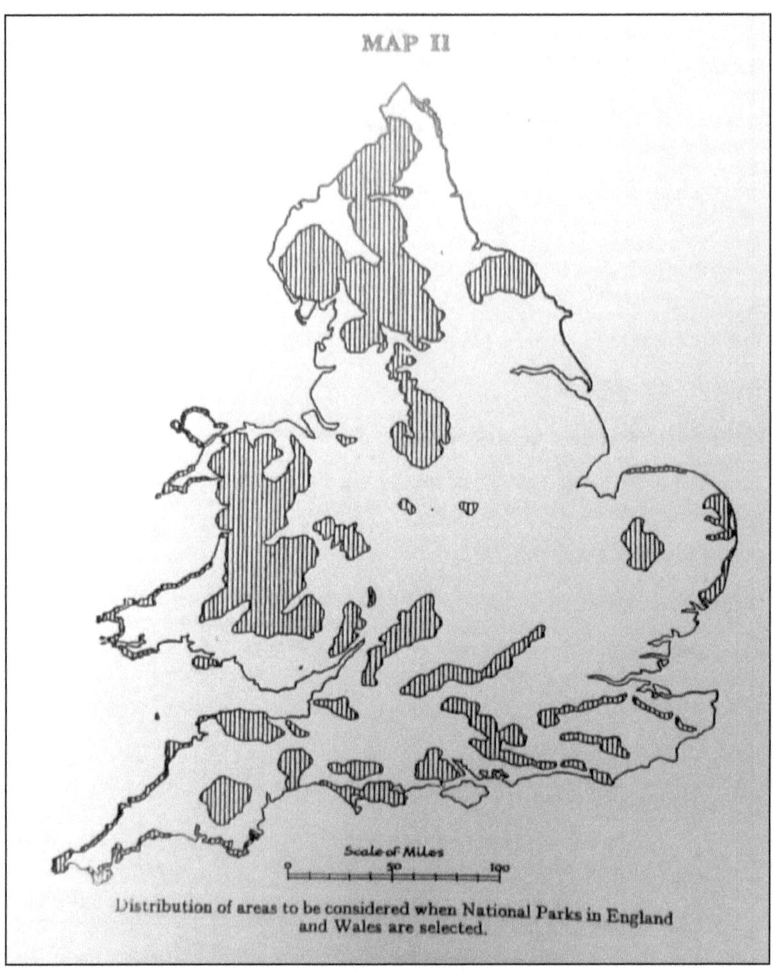

Figure 4: Dower's Map 2 Showing the 'Distribution of areas to be considered when National Parks in England and Wales are selected'

Chapter 1 - The Vision for National Parks

'On crossing the threshold, we pass into a charmed territory where everything shall be in harmony.' (Baille Scott, 1906)

'National Parks are a simple idea but an idealistic one; sweeping in scale, but potentially human.' (Purves, 2000)

The enactment of the National Parks and Access to the Countryside Act 1949 was the culmination of the vision for protecting England's finest landscapes as National Parks. Also, as it turned out in the Act, "Areas of Outstanding Natural Beauty", for securing the preservation of the special qualities of the landscape, and to meet the increasing aspirations of the access to the countryside movement. Whilst the case for establishing National Parks appeared obvious to the campaigners, especially in the 1920s, 1930s and 1940s, ever since, starting with some of the 1940s seminal reports, we have assumed that the case for designation was widely known and accepted. Indeed, so much was the case to establish the National Parks understood, and so much had it triumphed and had become absorbed by politicians, that John Dower, in his seminal Report which laid the foundations for the National Parks and Access to the Countryside Act 1949, reports '*the establishment of National Parks as part of the programme of post-war reconstruction – make it needless to embark here on any general argument of the 'case' for National Parks.'* (Dower, 1945). In the decades since the Act, the case has, never been fully articulated. This could explain the significant loss of wider public support for our landscape designations.

The history of the National Park movement and of National Parks in England, is often traced back to the thinking of William Wordsworth that the Lake District should become protected as *'...persons of pure taste...deem the district a sort of national property, in which every man has a right and interest who has an eye to perceive and a heart to enjoy.'* (Wordsworth, 1810). The context of Wordsworth and the Romantic movement is central to the cause of designated landscapes as George Treveleyan argues *'The modern attitude to natural beauty, more philosophic and more conspicuous, began, .. with Wordsworth, who gave it not only its first but its finest expression.'* (Treveleyan, 1931) Wordsworth's perceptive suggestion was an often-quoted comment in publications referring to the history of National Parks and the National Trust. Less often mentioned is where Wordsworth places this clarion call in the text of his *Guide*. This placement is fundamental to understanding the values we hold today for designated areas as they are underpinned by their cultural dimension. Wordsworth places this seminal phrase towards the end of his third chapter. First, he considers the natural forms and elements, the associative qualities such as light, which form the character of the area. Secondly, he traces the history of people in the area and how they evolved the living, working landscape, which he and others regarded as beautiful. By now in the *Guide,* we have an understanding as to how the works of nature and people have made the landscape so special. Thirdly, he looks at the changes affecting the landscape, many of which he disapproved, and his "rules" for preventing their bad effects. Whilst acknowledging the landscape has been changing over millennia there are some changes he sees as disfigurements and, as such, be resisted. In other cases, he acknowledges change should occur and suggests how it might be achieved to retain the special qualities of the landscape. Here comes his pivotal statement of a "*sort of national property.*" In short his preservation of the area was not about resisting any change but accommodating changes which reflected the special qualities of the area in which they were happening but resisting changes which detracted from the character of what we call now a cultural landscape. This point is fundamental for whilst we have exchanged the term conservation for preservation we are talking about managing the rate, scale, nature and direction of change. Wordsworth gave us this implied definition of conservation, which is still valid today. Preservation of the beauty and special qualities of the area should, in Wordsworth's view, be achieved by recognising the potential values such areas should have for the whole nation. It is these values, which his disciple John Ruskin, and his followers in turn, developed and applied to protect our finest landscapes.

The Wordsworth idea of national property was more readily absorbed overseas, especially in Australia, Canada and the USA, where governments obtained stewardship of large tracts of land, often 'virgin' territory, where Nature was paramount and where little human activity was apparent or readily removed. However, Wordsworth's idea of a National Park was for an area where the works of man existed alongside and with Nature. Today we would describe the position as sustainable with respect to economics, community, nature, and landscape. Keith Thomas suggests the changing context of the English mood that allowed such ideas to take root *'By the later seventeenth century the anthropocentric tradition itself was being eroded. The explicit acceptance of the view that the world does not exist for man alone can be fairly regarded as one of the greatest revolutions in modern Western thought,'* Thomas adds this mood involved the understanding *'There was no particular reason to think that either the earth or the human race was a particularly central part of the universe.'* (Thomas, 1983) Indeed, it was a railway Bill, the proposed extension of the Windermere branch line (which Wordsworth strongly opposed, despite being a shareholder!) to Ambleside, which first brought the words "National Park" into the Parliamentary record in 1877. An opponent of the railway Bill, James Bryce MP, said he had received abundant evidence of opposition to the Bill:

'not only from Lancashire and Yorkshire but even from the manufacturing districts of Northumberland and Durham. The people of those districts feel the greatest interest in the preservation of their piece of scenery. Now, the people look upon the Lake District as their National Park, and they desire to preserve it.' (Himsworth, pers. comm.)

This is the first governmental reference to National Parks, which extolled the working person's concern for the preservation of fine landscapes in which they wanted a freedom to roam.

The National Park ideas in England came to the fore of the public imagination during the campaign against Manchester City Council's proposal to dam Thirlmere into a reservoir in the late 1870s. Not only did this campaign give the public the right to protest about proposals that would damage the beauty of landscapes in which they had no legal title but also it led to a national sentiment for the enhanced protection of areas of great natural beauty for the nation.

The call for National Parks

During the Thirlmere debate *The Times* [20 October, 1877] concludes an article:

'When once the straight line of the embankment is harshly scored across the varied curves whose beauty has delighted many generations, when the millions have been spent and the quiet winding lake has swelled in to a tank with a ghastly margin of whitened stones all through the summer, it will be too late to regret that one more corner has been cut off from the narrow playground of Englishmen. We praise the munificence which spends thousands to provide People's Parks; surely it were well for us to husband the more exquisite Parks which Nature has provided gratuitously for our People.'

Wordsworth's call for a '*sort of national property*' had been restated, the challenge was down for the successors of the Thirlmere Defence Association (TDA). *The Standard* [2 November 1877] adds to this call:

'The beauty of the English Lakes is not the sole property of the landowners to whom the soil belongs. The mere fact that a man may own the barren land covered with scanty grass or profitless heather gives him no moral right to exclude his countrymen from the enjoyment of splendid scenery. ...If the landowner has no moral right to close these exquisite scenes against the present generation, still less is he entitled to mar their beauty for ever, and thus perpetuate as against posterity their offence which, with all their almost superstitious reverence for territorial property, Englishmen of to-day would not endure.'

This spirited call echoes Robert Somervell's pamphlet written for the TDA:

'Englishmen generally have a direct interest in the preservation of natural beauty of mountain districts, the value of which increases year by year with our increasing population, and the consequent rapid appropriation of the general surface of the land to purely utilitarian purposes.' (Thirlmere Defence Association, 1877)

Somervell, in setting out the case against damming Thirlmere, was to claim that it was not just from a self-interest of members of the TDA that the opposition to the Thirlmere scheme had arisen (this, it emerged, was only partly true). But it was, he claimed, in the interest of those who will come after us *'The sentiment of beauty in Nature, and the love of mountain scenery, have been much developed of late years, and are likely to increase in power and importance.'* (Thirlmere Defence Association, 1877). This foresight reflects how, for almost fifty years following the

1949 Act, most of the English and Welsh National Parks were in more mountainous areas.

This call for National Parks was enjoined by *The Yorkshire Post and Leeds Intelligencer* [2 January 1878]:

'There are two ways in which the desolation of advancing man can be prevented, namely, by such economy in work as to get riches from the earth without wasting its surface; and secondly, by setting apart districts which shall not be invaded by cities and destructive industries. In America, vast tracts of country by a foreseeing people have thus been protected for ever; and in England, by no foresight, but by good fortune, some such tracts still remain unblemished. Parks of recreation near our large towns are now provided at great cost, where labouring people and their children may come out and see the sky and the green tree, and to breathe the air of heaven. And beyond these yet remain still, greater peaceful areas - which, once rudely handled, are lost for ever. Such are, among other, the New Forest, North Wales, and the Lake country.'

The editorial continues on the Thirlmere campaign:

'But when Manchester to this end, propose to destroy the natural beauty of the choicest spot in Great Britain - to bring vast engineering works and desolation therewith into the loveliest playground perhaps in Europe - then we are bound to withstand such encroachments. ... The Lake country belongs in a sense, and that the widest and best sense, not to a few owners of mountain pasture, but to the people of England, and the Thirlmere Defence Association must be and is already a national association. It concludes, thankfully wrongly, *'If Manchester be allowed to have her unrestricted way at Thirlmere, there will be small hope for any future interference in the interests of the public.'*

Parliamentarian W.E. Forster, speaking at the time of the debate, notes *'We have in this part of England some of the most beautiful scenery in the world and it is the object of the House of Commons and of the country to preserve it.'* (HMSO, 1878)

The Manchester scheme, despite the public health benefits case made for additional water supplies to the city, was opposed by *The Medical Press and Examiner* [2 January 1878]. It balances these interests when it states:

> *'The Lake District is the national property of the people of England; it is the bounteous gift of Providence to them, all the more valuable in the present day for its rarity and its unique features. We know the value set on parks when in the neighbourhood of large towns; they are places for recreation, where our working classes can secure diversity of occupation, and pleasure from the artificial imitation of Nature's handiwork... But a still greater value should be set upon a succession of parks, fresh from Nature's hand, not the property of one town, but where every man can resort for change of scene, for the invigoration, in pure air, of his overtaxed energies; where the hardy son of toil and the fortunate possessor of wealth can extract equal pleasure from the contemplation of scenery unrivalled in its class.'*

The TDA and press campaign against Manchester's proposal stress two main elements -the value of protecting beautiful landscapes from the ravages of economic exploitation and of their enjoyment by the whole nation. These two elements, each with a varying set of ambitions and values, later formed the two major strands of the National Park movement and their parallel evolution is considered in the following two chapters. From the Thirlmere lost cause was laid the foundations of the British system of National Park administration and management, a unique system of control of non-publicly owned land, where a national interest in the aesthetics underpins the designation. The system might be currently under threat through government antipathy and under-funding but the establishment of a system without payment of compensation to private landowners for protecting public goods (still worthy of higher regard) became enshrined as a foundation of future claims for landscape protection.

Natural Beauty

There was another element to emerge from Thirlmere, which underpinned all future considerations of National Parks. Again, it was a unique piece of British conceptualism in the use of a highly charged term **natural beauty** as an appropriate presentation to describe our finest landscapes. The first written use of this specific phrase appears to be the petition to parliament (House of Commons Committee) in 1878 by the TDA when opposing Manchester's Bill. The term appears to have been established at this time, became enshrined in the 1949 Act establishing National Parks, and is still part of our current vocabulary for designated landscapes. In statutory terms, natural beauty was first used in the legislation of 1907 to establish the National Trust for Places of Historic Interest and Natural Beauty. As such, it still carries material weight for the current activities of the Trust. The use in the Thirlmere Defence Association petition suggests that Robert Somervell or his fellow worker W.H. Hills may have been the author.

George Trevelyan describes *'that vague phrase "the preservation of natural beauty".'* He values the concept with admirable clarity *'Yet what if that vague phrase stands for one of the most important of our national interests? What if "natural beauty" be one of England's greatest assets, spiritually and even, as I shall endeavour to show, financially?'* (Treveleyan, 1929). It was a phrase that he understood was complex:

'The appeal of natural beauty is not a single, simple thing. The aspect of nature varies from place to place and day to

day; and its appeal is made to the highly composite mind of modern man, which contains an infinity of aptitudes, tastes, desires, traditions, mysticisms, primeval inheritances and physical and physiological urgings, to all of which natural beauty makes, in a variety of ways, its strange and haunting appeal.' (Trevelyan, 1931)

Trevelyan argues because the phrase has no clear interpretation *'it does not lessen its value.'* It is, he says, *'the highest common denominator in the spiritual life of today.'* (Treveleyan, 1931)

Natural beauty is not, as many people today assume, used to describe untamed, self-willed landscapes in a way other nations define their National Parks. Some of our natural beauty does relate to landscapes and habitats where through geology or geomorphology and climate or works of people have had a relatively minor impact on the landscape. It includes privately owned land where farming and woodlands and sometimes industrial activities, have been instrumental in defining the surface appearance of the land over millennia. However, and this is what is crucial to our use of the word natural and to the understanding of the landscape conservation movement most of the works which affected the landscape had been gradual and cumulative over a long period. Significant changes in technology since the Victorian era and more particularly the drive of major economic development today at a rate and scale of change which, coupled with unsympathetic consideration by some developers towards natural beauty or their total unconcern for landscape aesthetics, often result in despoliation which can be the root of problems for the conservationist today. Trevelyan as an earlier exponent of this understanding notes *'A hundred years ago, just before the railway age began, this island was, almost all of it, beautiful, even more beautiful, perhaps, than it had been in its wilder state a thousand years farther back in time.'* He continues *'For man's daily work still supplemented nature's, without those harsh contrasts of line and colour to which we are to-day only too well accustomed.'* (Treveleyan, 1929). The English concept of natural beauty, for designated landscapes and nature conservation, is more about accommodating beauty within the everyday lives of people with the consent of people, a concept which other countries are now finding attractive for their designated areas. Such a concept can only be successful if consent is given with clear understandings of the values and benefits that are intrinsic to the phrase. The theory is, however, often better than the delivery. The lack of consideration for landscape aesthetics can be equally the greedy developer as it is the landscape preservationist who has forgotten to explain the values of 'living with' rather than in 'conquering' nature and natural beauty. The needs of less intensively used landscapes for the re-creation, inspiration and spirituality of the nation is perhaps greater today than at any time in our history yet it is the minor consideration of governments and of people who have become unnaturally divorced from landscapes of beauty. (Brodie, 2012).

William Wordsworth used the phrase 'native beauty" in his *Guide* (Wordsworth, 1810) but the key to understanding the derivation of the phrase natural beauty may lie in the passage he rejected for the *Prelude* Book 8 *'his favourite theme of the union of the child's imagination, through love and wonder, with the world of nature and the works of man.'* This perhaps takes us closer to what we in Britain understand by natural beauty, a working but symbiotic and respectful relationship with Nature. (Moorman, 1957).

Figure 5: Looking north from the Stipperstones, Shropshire Hills AONB

Twentieth-century evolution of values

The Great War, the recession of the 1930's and the Second World War all had a role to play in changing the social conditions and the social fabric of Britain. It is not surprising therefore that the main thrust for the designation of National Parks, and the more comprehensive exposition of why we need National Parks, was produced during this period. Writers in the immediate post-war period, as between the wars, were unequivocal in espousing the protection of landscape beauty as an urgent, primary human need. Harry Batsford is an example of the genre *'it is curious that the present age appreciate and enjoy beauty, and yet has to stand helplessly by while possessions are wrung from it.'* He should no doubt be more deeply concerned today as he continues:

> *'What is the matter with modern life, the past ages have created beauty of landscape and building, and we can do nothing but destroy them? There is something fundamentally wrong with the process of present day existence when in the regular march of events there may be swept out of existence*

most of what is gracious and pleasant that has come down to us.' (Batsford, 1946)

Even in the post-World War Two era such thoughts were not new and the concept of preserving and enhancing natural beauty can be traced through Rouseau, Wordsworth, Muir, Thoreau, Mill, Ruskin and other writers and thinkers of their day. Isabel Colegate reminds us of some of these influences:

'The solemn John Stuart Mill in 1848 wrote about the importance of preserving places where people could be alone. Solitude, in the sense of being often alone, is essential to any depth of meditation or character...solitude in the presence of natural beauty and grandeur is the cradle of thoughts and aspirations which are not only good for the individual, but which society can ill do without. Later on George Macaulay Trevelyan, the historian whose passionate support was one of the founding bases of the National Trust, did not regard solitude as something for poets and contemplatives only. He thought of it as a universal need, something which from time to time refreshed the spirit of all human beings and without which they were in danger of loosing touch with the springs of being.' (Colegate, 2001)

Wordsworth, Mill and their kind were not just suggesting preservation of landscape for their own nomadic ends but in the interest of a wider public. Albert Camus, albeit in a different context, made this link *'If I judge that a thing is true, I must preserve it.'* (Camus, 1942) To those who believed in the value of landscape beauty to humankind it became a fundamental truth. Camus realised why we campaign for beauty particularly during a time of war:

'All those who are struggling for freedom to-day are alternatively fighting for beauty. Of course, it is not a question of defending beauty for itself. Beauty cannot do without man and we shall not give our era its nobility and serenity unless we follow it in its misfortune. ... But it is no

less time that man cannot do without beauty and this is what our era pretends to want to disregard.' (Camus, 1942).

The English and Welsh, and more recently the Scottish, designation of National Parks are vastly more complex than and different from the application of the designation of the same name in most other parts of the world. Our development of the concept was at its height in the 1930s and 1940s, when the work of far sighted individuals such as John Dower and Arthur Hobhouse advising Government, alongside campaigners such as Cyril Joad, G.H.B. Ward, Tom Stephenson, Benny Rothman, Kenneth Spence, R.S.T. Chorley, Patrick Abercrombie and H.H. Symonds, revealed and brought to reality, the vision for National Parks in England. Such a vision was an integral part of our cultural heritage, our nationalism, our corner of western civilization that had evolved from our attraction to and, to a degree our repudiation of the Picturesque and, more vitally, the Romantic Movement at a time of sacrifice during the two World Wars. Cyril Joad notes *'The English countryside is a heritage of great worth that we have received from our ancestors; we owe it to them no less than to ourselves to hand it on undiminished to our posterity.'* (Joad, 1946) He adds, writing in a context of the understanding of the down-side of the increase in motoring and economic development, *'our age cannot create beauty, it should be more scrupulous to preserve the beauty which has come down to it. It is not, and destiny might have seen fit to be jealous on beauty's behalf.'* (Joad, 1946) Joad, two years earlier, he had succinctly argued *'This heritage which we have received from the past, we owe it to our ancestors to preserve and to hand on undiminished to our posterity.'* (Joad, 1944).

There was, however, a marked, but not entirely divergent, contrast between the main visions for National Parks; the campaigns for access and the landscape preservation movement. The timing of the enabling legislation in 1949, part of a new compact for rebuilding war weary Britain, was a recognition that the whole nation should benefit from a peace dividend in the protection of our best landscapes for which much blood was spilled in the conflict of the two world wars. There was at this time a ready acceptance that the British people could, in a number of ways, benefit significantly from the appropriate enjoyment of the natural beauty of these areas.

The threads of the National Park movement are largely identifiable as two separate strands with differing agendas yet with a common purpose to achieve legislation, which, however, proved to be a far from satisfactory response to their long campaign. Many of the aspirations and hopes to be incorporated in the National Park legislation are, as noted later (Chapter 4), still unmet. Arthur Blenkinsopp describes the National Park campaign as:

> '*a compound of different elements, although they were not exclusive. There were the conservationists (or naturalists) and their supporters.... Then there were the radical reformers who combined concern for access to privately-owned mountains and moorland with a romantic attachment to the countryside. And there were the millions of people who were beginning to escape out of crowded smoke-filled towns....*' (Blenkinsopp, 1975)

On one hand were urban ramblers whose vision for National Parks was inseparable from their Socialism and their urge for the necessity of escaping the confines of the polluted industrial towns where they toiled long and for little reward each week. On the other were the more middle and upper class aesthetes who wished to protect particularly fine areas of the countryside from the rapid urban developments that were affecting the rurality of the countryside as well as the rapid development of the urban fringe, and of unacceptably intrusive changes to sensitive areas of landscape.

For many in industrial towns the openness and freedom of the adjacent moorlands were denied to them and they saw the creation of National Parks as a concomitant to freedom of access to these relatively wild places. Rambling was a postponed gratification and a sustainable re-creation for the long hours worked in polluted and largely unsafe working conditions and enabled them an escape into the countryside as free men with a power of choice as to where they wandered. They might also dream that one day they might finally escape industrial pollution and breathe fresh air for both their health and their mind and spirit. Even today, we have to make a conscious effort to remind ourselves of the value of designated landscapes such as National Parks and areas of outstanding natural beauty to the national health, a further reminder that we have forgotten the vision for the establishment of such areas. The Ramblers' vision for National Parks is the subject of the next chapter, that of the landscape preservationists in Chapter 3.

The underlying common interest is for the designation of National Parks and areas of outstanding natural beauty, is the protection and the enhancement of the character of the landscape – the wilder, the natural and the cultural landscapes, which have been declared to be of importance for the health and welfare of the whole nation. The proponents of the vision were the largely articulate, educated strata of society who espoused more liberal values for the need to preserve the finest landscape from unacceptable changes. The influence of the Romantic Movement can be regarded as paramount but to the opponents of landscape protection, largely those who can profit most from unacceptable changes to the landscape, Romanticism is still used as a term of derision, largely reflected in the unsustainable cliché that conservationists want the landscape "preserved in aspic."

It should be understood that these two apparently separate campaigning threads were not just parallel worlds. The ramblers had their intellectual visionaries who readily accepted that landscape protection was essential to those who walked and experienced the countryside. The rambling movement had many fine writers, many working-class naturalists and geologists whose contribution to scholarship is still held in high regard. The common ground of preserving fine landscapes for appropriate, quiet re-creation was considerable, as was the recognition that these two strands might conflict. Leading ramblers' activist Tom Stephenson notes:

> *'The idea of limited access is a vestige of the Wordsworthian fear of the Lake District being invaded by hoards of untutored Lancashire mill workers incapable of appreciating nature in her more majestic forms. Like Wordsworth some people think that artisans and labourers should not be tempted to such scenery. ..The idea of protecting natural beauty and then prohibiting public enjoying of it is preposterous and impracticable.'*
> (Stephenson, 1989)

Stephenson may have misread Wordsworth's quote, made in the context of a railway proposal in the Lake District, but his worries were commonly shared. These worries, ignored today, are now phrased as a debate between designated areas being a National Park or a tourist resort. Stephenson's quote perhaps contained a point against an earlier leading compatriot in the access and amenity world Professor Cyril Joad, who entitled one of his books as '*A Charter for Ramblers*' and a second as '*The Untutored Townsman's Invasion of the Country*'! What was notable at the time of National Park campaigning was the number of leading proponents within the two movements who could comfortably and acceptably cross into the company of the other strand.

Tom Stephenson was one such link across the spectrum of the National Park movement. He was a civil servant and government press officer and, later, secretary of the Ramblers' Association, who categorised the interested national park proponents '*the National Park movement had its beginnings in several small runlets which merged into a main stream which eventually gained sufficient head to turn the mills of legislation. The four main tributaries comprise:*

a) the admirers of natural beauty,
b) the seekers of healthy exercise,
c) nature lovers and
d) later in the day the conservationists.'(Stephenson, 1989)

The threads of the National Park movement, whilst identifiable as separate strands with differing agendas, yet had a common purpose to achieve legislation, which Blenkinsopp describes as:

'*a compound of different elements, although they were not exclusive. There were the conservationists (or naturalists) and their supporters...Then there were the radical reformers who combined concern for access to privately-owned mountains and moorland with a romantic attachment to the countryside. And there were the millions of people who were beginning to escape out of crowded smoke-filled towns....*'
(Blenkinsopp, 1975)

Patrick Abercrombie and Sydney Kelly articulate the various strands in the context of their work in planning for the Lake District:

'*If this district is to be dedicated as a National Park or an area of national scenic importance it would appear that it should combine a threefold object; first, the preservation of scenery; second, the maintenance of flora and fauna; and third, the provision of recreation. Of these it might be suggested that the scenic aspect would involve as far as possible the preservation of the* status quo, *with the provision, however, of increased access in order that it may be enjoyed more fully.'* (Abercrombie & Kelly, 1932)

In his autobiographical account Stephenson celebrates *'the creation of National Parks, whereby large areas of beautiful country would be preserved for the enjoyment of the people and protected from the ravages of unplanned buildings, and the devastation of uncontrolled industrial development whereby the national heritage is sacrificed for private gain.'* (Stephenson, 1989) Stephenson regarded H.H. Symonds, a leading light of conservation bodies the Friends of the Lake District and the Standing Committee on National Parks, as the *'father of our National Parks.'*(30) Holt notes that Stephenson went further when he describes Symonds as *'the father of our National Parks and the finest intellect that ever served the R.A.'* (Holt, 1985). Arthur Dower, and G.M. Trevelyan were others whose views were well respected in both strands. The roots of the two main separate threads working towards the establishment of English National Parks thus set and are still prevalent today as shown through National Parks having two contrasting statutory purposes.

National Parks as War Memorials

'the England which men crossed the ocean to visit on account of its delicate beauty, the England to save which the young men went to die in the Great War?'
(Trevelyan, 1929).

The critical mass of support for the National Park movement was fostered in a specific window of history. The amenity movement gained strength after the Great War when the English character was undergoing fundamental changes in a spirit of peace whilst the old order of the Establishment sought to cling to its position of power. It was a search for a more natural, rural utopia in a country 'fit for heroes'. It was a time when the countryside, its ownership and its agricultural practices began to undergo fundamental changes. The case for National Parks can be read as being fostered in and reflecting too specific a window of history.

Following the Great War, alpinist and mountaineer Frank Smythe records *'Providence had designed a golden road of thought, a vision of the hills to illuminate the dark side-passages of life.'* (Smythe, 1935) The Great War had interrupted the access to the Alps for climbers and they came to associate the regaining of access to these mountains as the removal of the clouds of war and, with the same emotional response, affected feelings for the love and protection of the finest English landscapes. Trevelyan adds a complementary perspective *'Between 1915 and 1918 I knew a great many people whose daily occupation it was to be in danger of being shot among the Alps, yet who did not for that reason fail to appreciate their beauty.'* (Treveleyan, 1931) Smythe continues his mountaineering thoughts during the early stages of World War II:

> *'War may shake its thunder from the sky, but the hills sleep on. And so men see in hills an answer to their dreams, a serenity and a purpose reaching beyond every transitory hope and fear. In them the past, the present and the future of Nature and of Man are united in a single chord. For what other reason do our hearts stand still when first there looms over the horizon's brim their well-remembered forms, than that in them we perceive peace ourselves and our place in the universal scheme?'* (Smythe, 1941)

The shadow of this war and the planning for the post-war peace brought together the campaigners from all backgrounds, not always in co-operative harmony, to seek to campaign to establish National Parks. The 1949 Act came after a time in history, when man had moved from what Arthur Koestler regards as *'...to live with the prospect of death as an individual'* to a post-Hiroshima age. Now there was a growing recognition of the threat of nuclear war and global pollution where Koestler cautions *'mankind as a whole has had to live with the prospect of its extinction as a* ***species***'. Koestler continues '*we have been taught to accept the transitiveness of personal existence, while taking the potential immortality of the human race for granted. This belief has ceased to be valid. We have to revise our axioms.*' (Koestler, 1978)

In a post-World War era, National Parks and countryside protection and a consideration of public access to the countryside gave us the framework in which the English could re-consider their axioms. To a huge degree, this was a product of the experience of war itself. The Great War gave birth to Ralph Vaughan Williams' *Pastoral Symphony* and, as Jonathan Bate notes, Houseman's '*A Shropshire Lad was a prized possession in the knapsacks of thousands of men on the Western Front in the Great War because from title-page onwards it evoked a potent image of the England for which they imagined they were fighting.*' (Bate, 1991) Those soldiers did not fight so the landowners could keep them from rambling the mountains, moors and the general countryside, that they fought, arguably, for an England with countryside free and fit for heroes. Too rarely now, do we remember our National Parks and our limited freedom to roam is, if we are to continue remembering the sacrifice of the world wars, a fitting memorial to those who fought and died in protecting the freedom and the beauty of the British countryside.

Marion Shoard writes '*By the time World War II was underway, there was a widespread feeling that the iron grip of the landowner in rural Britain must have loosened ...It was widely accepted that among the policies of a post-war administration would be conservation of the countryside and the provision of access to it.*' (Shoard, 1978) Joad, notes:

> '*The National Parks, are mainly the concern of townspeople. There is evidence that interest is growing. Some of the men and women who have been compelled for*

five years to face the grim menace of invasion and death now desire to see the pleasant land for which they struggled, and out of their great love for it demand that its beauties be preserved, that the desecration of industrialisation, jerry-planning, the depredation of war, the enclosures by Service Department, and the dilapidations resulting from years of agricultural decline may all be remedied, and the right to roam freely over mountains, moors and uncultivated places may be enjoyed by the many instead of only a few.' (Joad, 1944)

Arthur Gardner made his claim for National Parks as an essential part of the post-war reconstruction and, in so doing, gave succour to the idea that our National Parks are still living war memorials. '*After all we must put first things first. When we have once supplied the bare necessities of existence, is it not more important to look after our minds and souls than mere luxuries for the body? The cultivation of our minds by the contemplation of the beautiful, especially when coupled with healthy exercise in the open air, should be valued more highly than the more expensive entertainments of modern civilization. Riches are only a means to an end, and are wanted for what they can buy for us. No man can spend more than a limited amount on his purely personal requirements, and beyond that what can he do better than provide himself with beautiful surroundings. Surely the nation should be ready to do this much!'* (Gardner, 1942)

If our designated landscapes and an ability to wander through the countryside are to be regarded as part of the peace dividend for sacrifice in two world wars then a whole sub-set of new questions should arise as to how we, today, might fittingly maintain those memorials.

Figure 6: Bury and Amberely Wildbooks, South Downs National Park

Development of the National Park idea

The Standing Committee on National Parks made out its case for such designated landscape in a leaflet published in 1938. Much of it is worth recalling:

'The rapidly growing demand for National Parks in Great Britain reflects three major movements of the present age: a revolutionary advance, through motor transport, in the power to get easily and quickly to even the remotest parts; a great increase in leisure through shorter hours of work and 'holidays with pay'; and a rapid extension among the mass of the people of a love of wild nature and a desire to visit and take exercise in beautiful and unspoilt scenery.'

Thus, the National Parks were seen as a protection against increasing urbanisation and a provision for the well-earned needs for re-creation of the nation. The pamphlet goes on to explain:

'Great Britain has a strictly limited amount of unspoilt country and there are many encroachments upon it – not only for week-end cottages, new or improved motor roads, car-parks, filling-stations, road-houses, advertisement-hoardings and all the paraphernalia that meet the needs of the 'country lover'; but also for such economic and public

developments as water-catchment, electric power schemes, artillery and bombing grounds, mining, quarrying, and commercial afforestation. To these rival demands the National Park movement opposes the triple claim of the lover of landscape beauty, the rambler and the naturalist. There is not a square mile too much of wilder country, and there is urgent need of a national policy for conserving the whole.... Behind all other claims lies that of the established farming use. The rough grazings which cover a large proportion of the wilder country form a vital element in the nation's agriculture of great actual – and still greater potential – value. With this claim the National Parks movement – unlike the various development demands – has no conflict and desires no interference.' (Standing Committee for National Parks, 1938)

These words were to be later and urgently retracted by the conservation movement when the UK government, and later European, subsidy ridden changes came about. These actions, such as the removal of hedgerows, the ploughing of downland, or the drainage of moorland, were to change significantly the appearance and natural history of the countryside following the more productive demands on the industry after the second World War. The claim, made in the pamphlet, is:

'The National Park movement asks (1) that a sufficient number of extensive and varied units, carefully selected from these potential National Park areas, should be strictly preserved and specifically run as National Parks; and (2) that the remainder of the potential National Park areas should be regarded as a reserve for further National Parks in the future, any development therein being permitted only if shown to be essential to the public interest.' (Standing Committee for National Parks, 1938)

The authors then explain the meaning of designation *'A National Park may be defined, in broad terms, as an extensive district of beautiful wilder landscape, strictly preserved in its natural aspect and kept or made widely accessible for public enjoyment and open-air recreation, including particularly cross-country walking, while continued in its traditional farming use.'* The pamphlet emphasizes such designated areas *'...must be of significance and service to the nation as a whole.'* The explanation continues:

'National Parks proper must further be distinguished from three associated purposes of great value, and of national significance, but with special characteristics and requirements. The first is the need for the creation of Nature Reserves for the strict protection of wild plants and animal life. ...It is indeed an essential part of National Parks policy that, wherever practicable, such strict Nature Reserves should be included within National Parks. ...Moreover, a general protection of wild life by suitable management and bylaws should be applied throughout National Park areas.' (Standing Committee for National Parks, 1938)

The document then speaks of the initiative to the creation of National Forest Parks and the need for coastal protection before it turns to Nature Reserves and the potential tension with open access *'It also throws more emphasis on public access, to some extent at the expense of Nature Reserve aspect; though observation of wild life should play a vital part in the recreational and educative value to the visiting public,'* (Standing Committee for National Parks, 1938)

The pamphlet continues:

'Moreover, National Parks are not merely a work of preservation – a purely negative task of preventing specific development or disfigurement; a positive side is equally necessary, not only to secure and increase access, ..., but also to preserve wild life and to maintain landscape beauty and effective farming use. For such activities the local

authorities have, in general, no mandate and no resources.' (Standing Committee for National Parks, 1938)

Joad comments cynically but not without some sympathy on the Standing Committee's definition as to the purposes of National Parks:

'This contains the heart of the matter; it brings out in particular the important point that the main principle which the concept of the National Park embodies is a negative one. The principle is, in fact, the principle of 'let alone'. The principle of 'let alone' means that an area such as the Lake District should be left in its natural state, left, that is to say, just as it is; that no steps should be taken to open it up, or make it easier for people to get there, or make it easier for people who ***have got there*** *to sit about in it or be carried about in it or to be entertained in it.*

Applied in practice, the principle means no villas, no wide concrete roads, no road houses, no elaborate pubs or smart hotels, no pylons, no sprucing and smartening up, no iron railings, no privet bushes, no advertisement hoardings. Local industries which do not disfigure the countryside, e.g. sheep farming in the Lake District and on the South Downs, pig and pony keeping and timber cutting in the New Forest, should be maintained, even encouraged; quarrying and mining should be prevented and, where they already go on, stopped.' (Joad, 1946)

A position too few connected with National Parks today would be brave enough openly to articulate. Adrian Phillips clarifies these sentiments:

'Let us be clear that none of the enthusiastic supporters of the National Park ideal, before or since 1949, envisaged a fossilized landscape, a museum to be visited by the rest of the populace. National Park landscapes have been shaped by man over the centuries, and that process cannot be stopped.

Moreover the people who live in the parks, though privileged by their ready access to beautiful countryside, are entitled to broadly the same material expectations of houses, jobs, transport and so on that the rest of us entertain.

But the National Park idea, as applied to England and Wales, makes no sense unless more weight is given to considerations of landscape conservation and access than in the countryside at large. The creation of National Parks was certainly intended to ensure the protection of those landscape and recreational features which brought their designation in the first place... Above all, National Parks make little sense unless the national importance of these areas is required to be recognized by all.' (Phillips, 1985)

Phillips is following the precedent outlined by the architect of National Parks John Dower. John Sheail reports on Dower's understanding of the negativity of protecting natural beauty:

'As Dower emphasized, it was not enough to give authorities strong powers to preserve the countryside from sporadic or ribbon development without any positive counterpart or means of enhancing town and countryside. People would not 'tolerate indefinitely a system which seemed to do nothing but restrict and frustrate their desires and enterprises'. Ways had to be found of accommodating larger numbers of people in the countryside, both for residence and recreation, without impairing rural values and landscapes.'

Sheail continues:

'Whilst Dower might describe his approach to landscape design as being one of conservation that ranged beyond the notion of preservation to encapsulate the concept of enhancement, it was imbued with a self-denying rather than a "self-assertive spirit". The inspiration was derived entirely

from what had been achieved by man and nature in the past. In the Lake District, he advised owners, architects, contractors and craftsmen to take as their guide 'the form and dispositions of the existing buildings, especially those of the seventeenth and eighteenth centuries'. This did not, however, imply a detailed and slavish imitation of the past...a core of basic characteristics corresponding to "the enduring facts of its natural and human setting." In such areas as the Lake District, the changes "should be of detail not of essence".' (Sheail, 1995)

Through the decades of having National Parks we have too often and too simply sat back as the negative process of development control has been seen as just that - a negative control. The reality of ensuring the positive attributes of the landscape are, through planning controls, being protected for the health of our and future generations is rarely, if ever, promoted.

Putting National in National Parks

The issue of control and management of National Parks has been a central issue throughout the movement from their creation and, more so, today. The Standing Committee was absolutely sure that in such designated areas *'A wide range of other functions, vital to an adequate National Parks policy, can only be performed efficiently if initiated, stimulated, guided, negotiated – some probably directly undertaken – by independent central bodies specifically charged with the task.'* (Standing Committee for National Parks, 1938)

National Parks were recognized as too precious to be left to the vagaries of local democracies whilst rural local authorities were regarded as too poor to fund National Parks in their districts. This was echoed in a pamphlet on *'National Parks'* issued, in the 1930s, by various amenity organizations and traditional providers of accommodation for the outdoor fraternity *'We must press the councils of the great cities to contribute to the cost, since it is for the welfare and recreation of their crowded populations that National Parks are most urgently required.'*(48) Today National Park authorities are being accused, not least by some of their more political members, as having a "democratic deficit" and are by no means nationally organised.

Lord Howard of Penrith, a northern Lake District landowner, had the view:

'There is of course nothing new in permitting lands to be taken over by the Crown for national purposes. What, however, is new to us…is that this safeguarding power of the Government should be extended in special cases, when a petition therefor shall have been proved to be well founded, to districts, places and objects for the purpose of preserving ***natural beauty or places of historic or scientific interest.***

Howard goes on to make a Platonic point, which, whilst still recognised, is greatly undervalued today:

'There is one other point that seems to me of supreme importance which is nevertheless often overlooked. This is the education of children in these matters. They need to be taught the value of the beautiful and the interesting things about them, that they may learn to appreciate them as part of their own prized possessions. Then it will be far more difficult for landowners who are vandals, for local authorities who are just ignorant, or even for Government departments (which are sometimes composed of philistines) to deprive us of such possessions as they may have done too often in the past."' (Howard, 1937)

Cyril Joad expressed a trenchant view as to the need for national control for National Parks:

'At present the wild areas in this country are under the control of Local Authorities, the assumption being that they are of concern only to those who live in the area. ... Now it does not occur to the Local Authorities who administer the wild areas to treat them as if they were national assets to be preserved for national use, nor, indeed, is the average Local Authority qualified to do so. Just because an area **is** *wild, it is thinly populated and the Local Authority therefore is poor. Therefore, it is usually without the means to operate such legislation as may exist for the protection of the countryside, legislation which is almost always permissive, hardly ever compulsory, nor can it afford to exercise such powers as it may possess to prevent the area under its control from being developed and ruined. On the contrary, just because it* **is** *poor, it seeks inevitably to attract the largest possible number of tourists to its area. It further desires them to be as rich as possible and it proposes, so far as lies within its power, to give them the kind of entertainment that they enjoy at Bournemouth or Blackpool. Thus Keswick clamours for a great by-passing motor road and plans its Winter Garden.*

Local Authorities are, after all, mainly composed of those townspeople who are tradesmen in the town. How can they not wish to make of the area under their control a vast pleasure ground, run on ordinary commercial lines and designed to attract the largest possible number of people who will spend their money in and about the town on the pleasures and goods that it pays members of the Local Authority to offer and to sell? The main objection to walkers is after all that they are such bad consumers.' Joad concludes his strong argument with *'In the case of the Lake District the difficulties that arise from Local Authority administration are complicated by the fact that the district as a whole falls within three separate County Councils, ...of eight Rural and three urban District Councils, and of eleven separate planning authorities who do not always see eye to eye. It is largely because of their disagreements that they have been unable or unwilling to take concerted action. For this reason, it is essential that the controlling authority for a National Park should be not a body concerned only with local interest, but a national body which, regarding the area as an asset to the nation as a whole, regards itself as responsible for the preservation of the nation's heritage.'* (Joad, 1946)

Even today, Joad would have found the position little different with five disparate local authorities covering the Lake District had a National Park authority not been established. Too frequently, these local authorities challenge the influence of a National Park body.

Arthur Gardner regards the principles of national park designation *'..regions are of outstanding importance in this connexion as they possess qualities of natural beauty beyond all the rest of the country, and their preservation becomes a national and not merely a local duty.'* (Gardner, 1942) Equally the 1930s saw a campaign for a system of planning to better manage change particularly in rural areas. Some felt that planning could obviate the need for designated landscapes. Planning legislation of 1947 gave additional powers to local authorities, which they had to consider surrendering to the newly created National Parks two years later. This blight is still with us today. However, the case for co-ordinated planning powers managed through National Parks has for a long time been recognized as essential. Gardner foresaw the problem:

'Planning, as we have tried to work it, has proved helpful in places, but its financial handicaps and weak handling have made it of little use in others. We have endeavoured to show that for the special conditions of the English Lake District it has proved inadequate, and that something more drastic will be necessary. ...What I am calling for in this volume is the realization of the supreme national importance of a few larger plans which are beyond the powers of local authorities or individual efforts. The dangers to which these

special areas are exposed are real and imminent, and if they are not faced the damage may be irreparable. We talk glibly of building up a new order and a better England, but the first step in this direction is to save what we can of the old England which we have loved. We must not let material prosperity blind us to the higher call of spiritual inspiration.' (Gardner, 1942)

At that time the Lake District area had a number of local authorities responsible for planning, who clearly demonstrated they were absolutely unwilling to work together to achieve a co-ordinated protection of the area. Indeed, it was not until 1974 that an appropriate degree of co-ordination was provided with the National Park authority having its own planning staff.

The Addison Report, whilst equivocal on many issues that would eventually affect National Parks, felt sufficiently strongly to record the unprecedented comment that National Parks should be areas which are *'large enough for the Nation to enjoy and important enough to justify the intervention of the state.'* (Addison, 1931) Yet there is always the dilemma expressed by Charlie Pye-Smith and Chris Hall *'We all have an interest in the land, the industrial labourer no less than the farmer. Individual freedom is one of the main considerations of political philosophy, and it can only exist if we all have the opportunity to participate in shaping the environment.'* (Pye-Smith & Hall, 1987)

Conflict between preservation and recreation

The inherent potential tensions in designating the protection of fine landscapes for the nation to explore had to be recognized early in the evolution of National Parks. Joad recognises the presence of people could possibly destroy the sense of wild and lonely places but asks:

'is it good that some places should be set apart where man may be assured of quiet and solitude and in face of the

grandeur of nature know the ways of the spirit and enter into possession of his soul?' Joad, not unexpectedly, readily answers his own question *'...all people and especially young people should be assured of the opportunities of occasional escapes from the trivial safety of our mechanical peace-time civilization; that the chance of adventure, even it may be danger, should be given to them so that they may feel the awe and mystery of the world. Such feelings come to men more easily in the mountain solitudes, especially when they have known fatigue and exposed themselves to risk, than anywhere in nature save, perhaps, in the desert or upon the sea.'* (Joad, 1946)

Dubos believes this tension was inevitable and insoluble:

'Various kinds of wilderness are being destroyed or spoiled all over the world. Laws may prevent exploitation or permanent occupation of wilderness areas, as in the case of National Parks, [the 'American model'] *but they cannot protect them against the damaging effects resulting from the mere presence of innumerable tourists. The phenomenal increase in public curiosity about certain wilderness areas makes it increasingly difficult to experience their qualities. The wilderness is thus another one of the worlds we are losing, in this case losing it as experience even though we preserve it physically.'* (Dubos, 1980)

John Sheail, reports the view of Dower on this matter *'Large numbers of people had to be admitted to the parks in order to justify the expense of protecting their beauty: at the same time, public access and recreational activities had to be carefully regulated, otherwise the parks would become 'neglected, blotched and evanescent', and this would ultimately be to the detriment of the visitors.'* (Sheail, 1995)

The English experience after many years of designated landscapes is primarily one where conflicting and modern demands for recreation have significantly affected the quality of experience of the traditionally recognised appropriate, quiet use of these wilder places, despite a few modest new controls, such as on off-road motor-vehicles, but proving only marginally helpful.

Agricultural use in National Parks

In some of the above statements, I have noted the understanding of the pre-war campaigners that the existing agricultural uses, mainly pastoral, would continue. In respect of woodlands we shall simply note that concerns over conifer afforestation did arise and were articulated. There was the underlying assumption that the landscapes of our finest landscape areas were evolved and maintained by traditional agricultural practices and there was no reason to change this perception.

Indeed the Justice Scott's Report of 1942 is notable for underlining this assumption and for allowing the minority report from Professor S.R. Dennison to demur from this otherwise rarely questioned and important fundamental principle. In short the National Park movement was grateful to and continued to expect the agricultural industry to continue after the war in the ways it had previously farmed.

Given the Scott Report was available to both Dower and Hobhouse the findings it has on agriculture are pertinent in considering the visions for National Parks. Scott recognises there is a need, for a wide range of reasons, to maintain and encourage a prosperous agricultural industry (see his paragraph 172 especially). Scott reports:

> *'The establishment of National Parks in Britain is long overdue. In so far as the character of the country it is desired to include within a National Park is determined by the type of farming (e.g. mountain sheep farming) it is essential for the form of utilisation to be continued with the proviso that in the case of a National Park it become*

secondary to the main purpose which is public recreation.'
(Scott, 1942)

Dennison, in his minority report, notes that whilst the majority believe land must be farmed in a traditional way if the *'amenities of the countryside are to be preserved'* (Scott, 1942), he would not press for the *'continuance and revival of traditional farming'* but would argue that to ensure prosperity in the industry there would need to be increased efficiency. Dennison continues that the main Report's emphasis on traditional farming techniques is because they felt this was the cheapest way to preserve the countryside. He warns that this can only be achieved at considerable cost. (Scott, 1942). Dennison has other pertinent arguments but the significant point today is that, whilst accepting the cultural nature of the landscapes of potential National Parks the Scott majority Report, did not foresee how post-war changes and different areas of government policy might impact on changed farming regimes and the landscapes considered for designation. This remains an issue of conflict between farmers and National Park authorities, and raises questions about how far National Parks (and possibly more appropriately National Park authorities) are fit for purpose.

Figure 7: Near Hatchett Pond, The New Forest National Park

Nor should we forget George Trevelyan's warning about not paying heed to the farmers *'That the unspoilt countryside is worth something also to its regular inhabitants, the downtrodden race of English agriculturalists, is another fact too frequently ignored.'* (Trevelyan, 1931)

Values in National Parks

The rural landscapes of National Parks are the places in England and Wales we best find superb places where human needs for truth, values and freedom can be met. Today a significant part of the desire to leave urban places to dwell in the countryside is because it is perceived that a rural location offers a better quality of life. The creation of the National Park ideal was a recognition that people who lived in towns and cities had the need to re-create in the countryside and so the two locations were, of necessity, inter-related. Pye-Smith and Hall state this fundamental *'Town and country are no longer separate entities which they once where, or seemed to be.'* (Pye-Smith & Hall, 1987) Joad recognised this in the aftermath of World War II '*He (the Countrygoer) cannot but think it right that the disinterested millions of the towns should be made free of the heritage of natural beauty which, incidentally, they have just been fighting to preserve.'* (Joad, 1945) The doughty defender of Dartmoor and its National Park Sylvia Sayer echoes this inclusiveness *'National Parks are not just a nice but slightly unnecessary and expendable luxury for a fortunate few. They are in fact a vital provision for a very real human need.'* (Sayer, 1970)

A nation state without ideals and the ability to articulate openly and without the ability to inculcate values of human relationships with quality countryside is of poor value for its population. New generations must be able to express openly other values for preserving basic human needs in the face of the pressures of mammon. The relationship with Nature, as a place of inspiration and of benefits to humankind, is not a new relationship but one that goes back to early civilisations as Cyril Moore reminds us:

'What little countryside we have to share between us is precious, and the freedom, no less than the capacity to enjoy it will have a profound effect upon the health and spirit of the future nation. At the lowest they are a necessary condition of a fitter nation. At the highest they touch the sources of national geniuses.' (Moore, 1944)

The National Park movement had to move forward on a pragmatic basis. This was to convince legislators of the need to establish landscape protection and enhanced access to wilder places through enactment. However, the people concerned with designated landscapes should not forget what Trevelyan expressed as: *'It is not a question of physical exercise only; it is also a question of spiritual exercise and enjoyment. It is a question of spiritual values. Without vision the people perish, and without the sight of the beauty of nature the spiritual power of the British people will be atrophied.'* (Trevelyan, 1937). Yet too frequently, those engaged in National Parks today forget or are loathe to be associated with, the fundamental reason for the designation of National Parks. This was to foster our health, happiness and spiritual quietude. They recoil from human emotional needs. Joad, in the context of writing about trees, came to a similar conclusion:

'This jaundiced vision is of a future which man, having conquered Nature, finds that in the process he has lost his own soul. For man cannot live by movies and radio alone, but by the spirit of God as it manifests itself in the visible scene that He has set before us in hills and valleys and rivers, in the air and the sky, in fields and flowers, in meadows and woods, and in great trees ranged in an avenue along a road or standing brooding and solitary in the fields. This exhortation to keep our trees is, then, in the last analysis a plea to preserve the conditions which are

necessary to our full human development as beings having minds and spirits as well as bodies and appetites.' (Joad, 1946)

All landscape within the designated area boundaries is not necessarily in harmony but we can protect and enhance that which is special to them. We have exquisite places and equally we should have high expectations of them '*That inscrutable quality of the True Romance......full of still quiet earnestness which seems to lull and soothe the spirit with promises of peace.'* (Baille Scott, 1906)

National Parks can be sacred places, where a person might own the soil but cannot own the spirit of the land. The spirit is the capacity to inspire people to treasure special memories. The designation of landscapes for their protection and enjoyment mediates between needs of society at large, and the value of special places to the nation. It might be asked whether without designated landscapes and the protection of and access to fine landscapes then personal values within our humanity could have perished. Harvey Taylor notes:

'A stance taken against the philistinism that sanctioned modern development in hitherto largely unspoilt natural environments – this was a specific focus of continuing concerns to the conservationist wing amongst countryside recreationists, which goes beyond the direct self-interest of today's so-called 'Nimby' phenomenon.' (Taylor, 1997)

It certainly does, but more fundamentally and more important, it goes to the heart of the future of our relationships with our fellow beings and with our place within Nature.

Post war changes to the needs of society

Arthur Gardner, in common with his contemporary commentators, saw National Parks as very special places and not for the provision of all entertainments *'A National Park is needed as a refuge from the noise and bustle of modern life, and those who can only enjoy themselves in crowds should be encouraged to go to places that cater for their tastes.'* (Gardner, 1942). That was not to say Gardner and others did not recognize that without a suitable economy we could not sustain the population or the countryside. He adds, with Platonic assertion:

> *'The problem before us is how to restore some measure of economic prosperity ...without spoiling the natural beauty which forms the best asset of the country. In the last century the study of economics was carried out on purely material and utilitarian lines without proper allowance for human nature and the need for higher things of life: the result was ..., the monotonous suburb, and a degraded population with a residue of hopeless unemployed. Since then we have partly woken up to these abuses and some of the worst of them have been removed or at least palliated, but we have still a long way to go before we can build up the Britain we should like to see. If we are to make better men and women we must provide for their souls as well as their bodies; we must bring them up to appreciate decent surroundings and natural beauty. Then only can art and music and the joys of the spirit flourish, and a nobler and greater people spring up.'*
> (Gardner, 1942)

A frequent response, in the days of slow agricultural changes, was to regard the English hills as inviolate and everlasting and, in the designation of National Parks to enshrine them as repositories for our beliefs, standards, values and ethics. Since then the world has moved on. Have National Parks values also changed? Are we at a position represented, albeit in a different context, by Albert Camus *'If men cannot refer to common values, which they all separately recognize, then man is incomprehensible to man?'* (Camus, 1951) Such is a difficulty of our current National Park movement in a different age from their foundation campaigns and when their agendas are, all too often, defensive reactions to the dominating power of the economic development lobby.

Today we too rarely hear the arguments for having and appropriately stewarding National Parks with their largely special values for society. Are we too arrogant to feel that such a case needs to be put or do we feel that the battle was won in 1949, and we can still rest on our laurels? Do we really have the public support necessary to build on the vision of those who established the National Parks in England? Can we readily articulate the reasons why we need National Parks more today than ever before? Alternatively, are they no longer a necessity for modern society? Certainly, in the 1920s, but more particularly in the 1930s and 1940s we readily heard the case and the vision for the establishment of National Parks. Today we hear only of the problems, mostly from a vociferous minority who would gain financial advantage if the designations were weakened or removed. Increasingly we hear from within of an insecurity of a concept, which can appear dated.

We have had National Park legislation since 1949 and still too many residents, local authorities, governmental bodies, businesses and visitors do not or do not want to know about the intrinsic value for the nation of these most special areas. Rene Dubos observes *'Most of us are ambivalent about defining environmental quality. Our attitudes are governed more by habit than by logic; they put us either in league with nature or in conflict with it, depending upon our past experiences and what we mean by the whole conservation and preservation.'* (Dubos, 1980) Is it that National Parks have only been discovered by marketing people and by the tourist industry at large? Are they now to be no more than tourist resorts based on marketing and profit taking?

Today, scarred from decades of attack after having, to a varying extent, stewarded against the continually increasing erosion from economic interests and, to a much lesser extent, the more urban demands of rural communities, the National Parks are being increasingly marginalised by the pressures from vested interests. The founders of the National Park movement saw them as areas to be regarded as inviolate, to be preserved and their special qualities to be enhanced for future generations. Decades of long-term vision have been and continue to be sacrificed to short-term materialism, and the values we originally associated with these beautiful landscapes continually have to be fought over, perhaps discarded.

A. Holmes advances the argument *'National Parks are more necessary to the crowded populations of England than any other country in the world.'* (Holmes, 1930). The urbanised population need guaranteed breathing space. Since 1949, the population of England has significantly grown; it has become more urbanised, more materialistic, more destructive, and more mobile as families move around the country for employment or social reasons. This mobility has led to a loss of roots, it is now harder for many people to identify with a familiar landscape in which once they would be born, grow up, live and die. The loss of that support has removed the emotional comfort of a sense of place in which people could feel they belonged. People have developed a shorter-term relationship with the landscape and one where economic factors have added a layer of opacity. This more footloose population with no long-term sense of place or belonging loosen also their commitment to citizenship and develop a changed attitude to stewardship of the landscape. Gone is the time to stand and stare and to understand the seasons that once were influential on our lifestyle. Our relationship with nature has been lost and replaced by surrogate activities. These are often technological, which serve to isolate us further from the values we can still discover in our countryside.

Such a hypothesis will not stand-up alone; society is much too diverse for that. Equally, there are more people walking the fells and field-paths than previously. The explanation of the loss of commitment to respect for landscape and an understanding of the need to protect such landscapes is more complex.

Figure 8: Ingram Brough Law to Cushat Law, Northumberland National Park

Chapter 2: The National Park Vision – access for walkers

People *'...need the refreshment which is obtainable from the beauty and quietness of unspoilt country. Since, therefore, it is not possible to sterilize great tracts of land, ..., it is all the more urgent to ensure that some at least of the extensive areas of beautiful and wild country in England and Wales are specially protected as part of the national heritage, that their use for popular enjoyment and open-air recreation is encouraged.'* (Hobhouse, 1947)

'Extensive tracts of countryside by reason of (a) their natural beauty and, (b) the opportunity they [National Parks] afford for open air recreation having regard to their character and to their position in relation to centres of population...should be subject of special measures to protect and enhance their natural beauty and for the promotion of their enjoyment by the public.' (National Parks Act, 1949)

National Park purposes are *'to conserve and enhance their natural beauty, wildlife, and cultural heritage; and to permit opportunities for the understanding and enjoyment of the special qualities of the National Parks by the public.'* (Environment Act, 1995)

Ramblers and kindred recreational activity bodies supported the designation of National Parks as this was regarded as a means to meeting their demand for greater access to mountain, moor, lakeshore, riverbank, downland and crag. Yet it was not this simple. In essence there was an amalgam of political reasons, underpinned by the common vision for greater access to the outdoors, which was unreasonably, staunchly and resolutely refused by a lobby including landowners, water supply authorities, grouse moor shooters, anglers, and tenant farmers. This lobby would still be present following the creation of National Parks. Nor were ramblers the only recreational group that sought greater access. Such a move was supported, albeit in smaller numbers and less vociferously, by cyclists, canoeists, rock climbers and field naturalists. However, it was the ramblers who were, and to whom the quote borrowed from Irving is most appropriate, '*...the bearers of an incomparable tradition.*' (Irving, 1935)

The formation of the Lake District Defence Society (LDDS), mainly through the efforts of Canon Rawnsley, in 1883, saw its draft prospectus continue the claim for the Lake District to be a National Park and states *'The English Lake District is becoming each year more and more the resort of all classes for health, rest and recreation.'* (CCC Archives, DSO24/9/1) The LDDS fought for both National Park recognition and the rights of people who sought access to the Lakeland countryside. (see Cousins, 2010 & Brodie, 2012)

This was a time when a significant proportion of ramblers were urban dwellers and when, according to George Trevelyan, *'in our time, most people live buried deep in ugly towns, removed from every natural sight and sound save for a strip of sky far overhead and the swish of rain on dirty streets.'* (Trevelyan, 1931) The urban ramblers' vision for National Parks, often inseparable from their socialism and who had a vital need to escape the confines of the polluted industrial towns where they laboured long each week. Theirs was a vision of escape to the hills, the freedom to roam on the moorlands and mountains of the landscape that enveloped their home towns, land they saw as future National Parks. They saw rambling partly as a reward for their postponed gratification from constrained hours of their industrial ties from where they could 'escape' into the countryside to behave as free people with a power of choice as to where they wandered. For some the choice would be determined by a long walk between public transport. For the often self-taught naturalist the need was to reach special habitats, and it was such people who added so huge an amount of information to the understanding and development of natural history and, eventually, to nature conservation in Britain. Howard Hill linked the demands of walkers for relaxation and leisure in the open air with the growing industrialisation of the nineteenth century. Many of those industrial towns were in close proximity or within easy public transport access to the open fells and moors where there was potential for National Park designation. It was, says Hill '*a growing revolt against urban existence.*' (Hill, 1980) This message has been a constant mantra in the establishment of National Parks. Arthur Gardner wrote of the hope and possibility of *'men working in those desolate and hideous towns to escape for holidays or weekends, for a breath of fresher air and a glimpse of the unspoilt face of nature.'* Gardner, 1942)

Sir Charles Trevelyan's speech to the 1937 CPRE Countryside Conference resonates with Government thinking of the day:

> *'The Government is at present engaged in a health campaign. It undertakes to assist the health of the nation and to find playing fields in the vast cities to play cricket and football. But it is no less essential for any national health scheme to preserve for the nation, walking grounds and regions where young and old can enjoy the sight of unspoilt Nature. And it is not a question of physical exercise only, it is also a question of spiritual values.'* (CPRE, 1937)

This theme of holidays for the urban citizens was taken up by R. G. Stapledon. He writes we must:

> *'provide facilities for rural holidays to the urban worker on a grand scale. For the latter purpose National Parks are an absolute necessity. By a National Park we must envisage something altogether different from a reserve. Something far more than a sanctuary for wild flowers and wild birds; not merely a breeding place for polecats, weasels and badgers, but a place where rational beings can do things and enjoy*

themselves in the country. Within a National Park by all means let us have small sanctuaries for wild things – birds and flowers in particular. Such sanctuaries, however, and the preservation of national monuments, excellent aims in themselves, are of relatively little importance compared with the provision of healthy (healthy to mind and body) holiday facilities for the urban masses amidst truly country surroundings – surroundings that are in no wise urbanized.' (Stapledon, 1937)

Stapledon can be accused of patronising the working classes and of misunderstanding the wider concept evolving as to what might constitute the ethos for National Parks but he was at least in tune with the national concerns for the then standard of urban living – he wrote at a particular time and place and his analysis appears strangely dated.

In a wider context Vaughan Cornish regards the potential creation of National Parks and the preservation of natural beauty as being *'essential to the national well-being.'* (Cornish, 1937), Lord Horder of Ashford argues:
'The preservation of the Amenities Front is vital for two reasons: First, because the conditions of modern life make it more important than ever before that we should do all we can to counteract the results of hustle and anxiety and competition. And it is vital because the fear connected with international insecurity exercises such a paralysing effect upon so many of the movements designed to increase human health and happiness, that it is essential we should combat this fear.' (Horder, 1937)

The Ramblers' and their ilk could rightly dream they might remove themselves from the industrial pollution that accompanied their working and everyday lives and go and breathe free, fresh breezes of health. We still too often, as many have before, continue to undervalue the role of National Parks, of AONBs, and other rural areas as a significant contributor to the national health, an error that today holds increasing interest more often regarded as a hook with which to align the movement with current government policy and to appear as main stream. In some limited respects the National Park movement could be construed as a contributory movement towards a National Health Service but one where prevention was better than cure.

This is not to forget the Ramblers' lobby did have their intellectual visionaries including those who viewed the countryside not only as a physical activity but as a political, social and spiritual re-creation. The rambling movement developed and produced many fine thinkers, writers, naturalists and geologists. They had G.H.B. Ward, Professor Joad, G.M. Trevelyan, Tom Stephenson, Phil Barnes, Gerald and Ethel Haythornthwaite, H.H. Symonds, and Lady Sayer amongst others. They, along with many other walkers, shared the re-creation and the spiritual visions. Nor is it an argument that two tribes, with recreationalists on one hand and conservationists, landscape protectors and nature conservationists on the other, had no common ground between them – they equally sought to protect fine landscapes and to make them available for quiet, appropriate re-creation. Equally, though simplistically, they foresaw that such a twin approach of conservation and access might, in certain circumstances, lead to a conflict within their mutual interest. But there was an increasingly shared recognition that people should not be denied the sight of nature.

The history of the rambling movement, of the Ramblers' Association, and the access movement is well documented. See for example Stephenson, Hill, Shoard, Holt, and the Sheffield Campaign for Access to Moorland. (see Hill, 1980) The major focus of the history of rambling in Britain is the coming together of differing rambling groups, often with tensions from a major north-south of England divide, to form a single voice to campaign for access to open countryside and for better protection of the system of public footpaths. It should not be forgotten that at the time of the campaign for National Parks the Ramblers' were, compared with current times, one of a relatively few national amenity organisations, with the Council to Protect Rural England (CPRE), Standing Committee for National Parks (SCNP), Friends of the Lake District (FLD), Youth Hostels Association (YHA), Commons and Open Spaces Society (OSS), Countrywide Holidays Association (CHA), Holiday Fellowship (HF), and Cyclist Touring Club (CTC) for example displaying varying degrees of kindred-spiritedness. These were largely voluntary in organisation, some of which have since undergone name changes, with paid staff arriving later. Some individuals such as Tom Stephenson, H. H. Symonds, Norman Birkett, Gerald and Ethel Haythornthwaite, H. Griffin, Lawrence Chubb, and Kenneth Spence, along with some MPs, provided important inter-organisational linkages, although it is generally regarded that such linkages were too few. Stephenson, who was national secretary of the Ramblers' Association (RA) describes the man most strongly associated with the Friends of the Lake District, H. H. Symonds, [pictured right] as *'the father of the National Parks movement and the finest intellect that ever served the R.A.'* (Holt, 1985) However they were not without personality clashes nor had they all the same dynamic spirit or skills to push a campaign for National Parks. Indeed not all the recreational bodies, as the Ramblers' found at their 1929 Leicester conference, favoured a public right of access to uncultivated mountain and moorland.

This history, whilst fascinating, is not directly relevant here, nor is there a necessity to focus on the well documented campaigns for access. It is the vision for National Parks that arose from the access campaign that is vital to our current and future understanding of the purposes of National Parks. The wilder areas of countryside where access was being sought were essentially the same places as the high quality landscapes for which National Park status would be claimed by all supporters of designation. In an inter-linking respect it is not easy fully to tease out the access from the National Park campaigning especially when a number of the ramblers' leaders were equally at home with the cause of landscape preservation. Hill reminds us:

> '*The Open Air Movement has become a major social phenomenon of many industrialised countries during the twentieth century. Having started as a mere trickle around the middle of the nineteenth century, it now embraces millions of ordinary people, many of whom have joined together into organisations catering for the varying needs of their outdoor activities.*' (Hill, 1980)

Despite the kindred spirits however, the achievement of designating National Parks in 1949 did not resemble to any reasonable extent the vision of the access campaigners, although it did enable the making of a very limited additional access to the mountains and moors achievable.

Figure 10: Dovedale, Peak District National Park

Howard Hill celebrates the fact that the achievement of the designation of National Parks and the freedom to roam largely avoided any significant confrontation between differing interests. This he explains:

'*Though all sections of the open-air movement have campaigned for both National Parks and access, noticeable are the social distinctions between those who have formed the leadership core in these respective campaigns. It has been the professional and semi-professional strata who led the National Parks movement, while on access it was the ordinary ramblers drawn from the industrial towns of the North. There are those who have attributed to these social distinctions the greater success of National Parks than of access. But this is to misread the situation. ... It is in this area [the Peak District] where the struggle for access was the fiercest and most sustained, without which it is doubtful whether National Parks would ever have come into existence.*' (Hill, 1980)

Hill forgot the degree of shared commonality of personalities and interests between the amenity and access sides of the open-air movement, especially out-with the Peak District.

Professor G M Trevelyan addressing the 1937 CPRE Annual Conference says:

'*The longing, too often a thwarted longing, for natural beauty and the great unspoiled spaces, is the most touching and a most hopeful thing in the modern city population. The condition of any real value in modern city life is holidays spent in the country.... With shorter hours of work, holidays with pay, and increasing leisure for millions, the question of the proper use of leisure has become a national problem second to none in importance. And it makes the provision of National Parks increasingly and urgently necessary....*' In his definition of a National Park Trevelyan includes '*...kept and made accessible for public enjoyment and open-air recreation, including particularly cross-country walking, ...*' (CPRE, 1937)

The parks were seen as places for quiet recreation appropriate to the grandeur of their surroundings. They were not proposed for any intrusive recreation – an ideal fully understood during the passage of the enabling Act of Parliament. Patrick Abercrombie and Sydney Kelly note in the particularly fine landscapes of Lakeland:

> *'Indiscriminate opening up for access by all type of machine is also equally foreign to the real use of the district for recreation.'* They add *'As regards to the recreative object, it is perhaps sufficient to say that in fulfilling this as completely as possible nothing should be done to destroy the very purpose for which people in search of recreation visit the lakes. Thus sounds like an axiom or a platitude, but there are persons quite capable of using the lure of natural beauty to attract the public and then debauching that beauty to appeal to the public's lower instincts.'* (Abercrombie & Kelly, 1932)

Cyril Joad succinctly argues the case for a freedom of access within the potential National Parks:

> *'The plea for 'access' is usually coupled at gatherings of ramblers with the demand for National Parks. On what grounds is this demand based? Primarily on the ever-increasing encroachment upon the wild country of England by the towns, or rather by their sprawling extensions. ...For the present it is sufficient to say that the floods of houses complete with inhabitants let loose since the War upon the surface of England make solitude ever more difficult to attain. You have to go further to find it, and it is harder to find when you have 'got there.*
>
> *...Modern men and women are like taut strings, for ever braced; we dare not relax for fear lest, should we fail to maintain the alert tension of our lives, we should miss the boat of pleasure or opportunity and drift to boredom and disaster. Yet, if we are to live easily and well, occasional*

relaxation is a necessity, and not only relaxation, but relaxation in solitude. That men and women have an instinctive need for country sights and sounds and an instinctive craving for occasional solitude are facts of which the most cursory study of psychology should convince us. These are the needs which the conditions of modern life make it increasingly difficult to satisfy. Hence the demand for National Parks.

...From these the sportsman and builder would be alike banished and the inhabitants of this overcrowded island would be assured of a set of retreats in which they could enjoy Nature and solitude broken only by the companionship of wild things.' (Joad, n.d.)

During the House of Commons debate of the National Parks and Access to the Countryside Bill the Rt. Hon. Lewis Silkin, with ideological conviction but coloured with a poetic flight of political language, says:

'it is perhaps a reason for our country's greatness that in a difficult period like the present we are not afraid to set aside time and energy for the practical measures needed to help people enjoy these beautiful areas.... Now at last we shall be able to see that the mountains of Snowdonia, the lakes and the waters of the Broads, the moors and dales of the Peak, south Downs and the tors of the west country belong to the people as a right and not as a concession. This is not just a Bill. It is a people's charter – a people's charter for the open air, for the bikers and the ramblers, for everyone who loves to get out in the open air and enjoy the countryside. Without it they are fettered.....with it the countryside is theirs to preserve, to cherish, to enjoy and to make their own.'
(Hansard, 31 March, 1949)

Even since the Access and Rights of Way Act of 2000, opening up some of our mountain, moorland, downland and common land to open access on foot, we are still waiting for

Silkin's pledge to be delivered in full. For example some 46% of the Lake District National Park is open access land but more should have been mapped.

Vaughan Cornish gave evidence to the Addison Committee in which he *'...praised Snowdonia and urged that it should be preserved as a pedestrian paradise and not 'opened up' for motor roads or organised recreation.'* (Federation of Manchester Ramblers', 1929) Thus National Parks were seen to be for informal, quiet recreation appropriate to the high quality landscapes. Yet, for the first fifty years of the designation of National Parks many were in the uplands where access was most sought. Yet access to much of these areas was not much enhanced until legislation in 2000 (see above) and, if we examine the proportion of designated landscape to which the public had full access to wander at will it still today falls woefully short of less than half the designated areas.

The vision for upland and National Park access was no mere seeking of physical pleasure. The Hobhouse Committee Report states:

> '*Fostered by the instincts of an urbanised population, torn increasingly from its ancient roots in the soil by the industrial revolution, an urban existence that pushes the primeval background out of sight, that makes it remote and unavailable, that deprives people of intimate contact with it [fine landscapes]...is unlikely to produce adequate men and women.*' (Hobhouse, 1947)

This is a reflection of the congruence between those who sought to preserve fine scenery and those who wanted fine scenery to be appreciated by all, achievable through appropriate, quiet recreation.

The access movement and the antagonism of landowners

An important pioneer of the access to mountains movement, Edwin Royce, records his view on the quality of candidate National Park areas such as the Peak and Lake Districts, areas where the long delayed public access to mountains and moorland he hoped would be achieved *'The serious obstacle to National Parks in this country is the shooting interest. Today we can assert that these lands are particularly suited to the varied purposes served by National Parks,'* Royce regards the shooting interests' *'selfish demands'* which made such people *'unfit for their stewardship and selfish demand to enjoy the exclusive use of such lands.'* (Federation of Manchester Ramblers', 1929) Here we can pick up the nub of the problem. Whilst some landowners wanted National Parks to protect the beauty of the areas, the needs of ramblers was one that conflicted with their interests in ownership of land that might be designated as a National Park. The politicisation of the access movement was therefore an anathema to them and here lies the root of the two-strand approach to the designation of National Parks and to their two statutory purposes. Tom Stephenson comments on the issues of problems stemming from over-zealous public landowners:

> *'In the proposed National Parks in mountain and moorland districts large areas of the best scenery formed [water] gathering grounds. It was inconceivable that wild uncultivated land within National Parks should continue to be forbidden territory. It was just as inconceivable that land of that type owned or controlled by public bodies should be less accessible than areas privately owned.'* (Stephenson, 1989)

Cyril Joad also comments on the increasing conflict and politicisation of the access movement and land ownership:

'Now there is no doubt in my mind that this new militancy among walkers is a growing thing. There is real resentment in the north at the monopoly of the moors, and a new note of urgency has in recent years crept into the ramblers' protests. Something of the intransigence of the politics of our time is reflected in this new attitude. On this, as on other issues, people are less inclined than they were to wait for the conversion of public opinion, more inclined to take the law into their own hands, when the community seems unwilling to satisfy or incapable of satisfying what they consider to be just demands. And so that well-known law-abiding timidity of walkers is gradually becoming a legend rather than a fact.' (Joad, n.d.)

Joad adds later:

'There are many persons belonging to the unemployed rich class, whose conception of the good life consists in depriving the other creatures of life. That the desire of 'sportsmen' to insert pieces of metal from a distance into the bodies of grouse and pheasants should be permitted to prevent citizens as a whole from walking on moors and in woods seems to me offensive to morals and repugnant to common sense. I profess myself totally unable to see any reason why the gratification of the tastes of a few rich men should be allowed to obstruct those pursuits of the many which, if I am right, constitute an integral part of the physical and psychological well-being of the community.' (Joad, 1937)

This attitude was not new for, way back in 1908, Arthur Ransome writes:

'Instead of the hereditary (sic) owner, I imagined the people. Instead of the private park, I imagined that I was walking through and enjoying a National Park, a kind of English 'Yosemite'. Why not? If we, under our present miserable economic system, can afford to allow one man to own and to use such a park, surely the People who owned all the land,

nationally and not individually, could afford to indulge in such a luxury.' (reported in Taylor, 1997)

With such positions it is more difficult to understand why the more middle-class orientated National Park landscape protection movement should find common cause with National Parks for a freedom to roam, more working-class movement. But such was, and still largely is, the politics of the English countryside even if the underlying attitudes of people and their social and political affiliations have changed over the decades.

For Dower this was simply an issue of the interests of the many over the few and that sooner or, as it turned out, later walkers should have a freedom to roam over grouse moors. A restored ancient right which still rankles with grouse moor owners.

Government reports on access and National Parks

Notwithstanding his pivotal role in government, the National Park movement and the Ramblers', Stephenson believes the question of open access was the less widely recognised of the two problems of the *'preservation of the remaining natural beauty of Britain and the obtaining of a general right of access to that beauty.'* (Stephenson, 1989) Stephenson notes the Dower Report and concludes *'there must be a right to wander at will over the whole extent of uncultivated land.'* (Stephenson, 1989) The earlier, first report into National Parks, by the Addison Committee, according to Stephenson *'had little to say of any value on the subject of access to uncultivated land.'* (Stephenson, 1989) and ramblers *"were not conspicuous on the Committee and its report shows little evidence of the consideration having been given to 'the improvement of recreational facilities for the people.'* (Stephenson, 1989) although Addison did pay some recognition to the public need for enhanced access to areas of natural beauty (see below).

Yet the Ramblers' federations had presented evidence to the Addison Committee, as Stephenson reports they suggest *'that a National Park should be large enough to furnish at least the greater part of a days walking –say, twenty miles.'* (Stephenson, 1989) and this should be in open country and on rights of way but avoiding towns and metalled roads. It should be noted that one of the four objectives set for the Addison Committee was 'measures for improving the recreational facilities of the people'. However, very early in the Addision Report we find:

> *'There is another side of the problem which should be mentioned. We have been told of damage inflicted by thoughtless individuals on both public and private lands to which they now enjoy access, and it has been pointed out that the grant of an unrestricted right of access for the public would depreciate the economic values of some lands, e.g., sporting areas and grazing lands, would involve a menace to public health in water catchment areas, and might be inimical to the preservation of flora and fauna, and even to the preservation of natural characteristics.'* (Addison, 1931)

The Committee went on to record:

> *'The question of improving the opportunities of access to the countryside for these (recreational users) and other sections of the community does not present the same urgency, over a large part of the country, as the question of preserving the countryside from disfigurement. The attitude of private landowners towards the public is generally liberal, and where access to areas of national interest has been denied or confined to certain tracts it is usually because a more general degree of access would be inconsistent with the use to which the land is put.'* (Addison, 1931)

So they nailed their attitude in respect of general public access to that of the shooters, water gatherers and major landowners who wanted no truck with the "great unwashed". The Committee concludes with a very minor concession:

'We do not, however, share the view expressed by some of our witnesses that the improvement of the recreational facilities necessarily involves the acquisition of an extensive scale of areas over which the public would have the right to roam at large. ... We think that the assistance should be provided by improving the opportunities of access for pedestrians to areas of exceptional natural beauty. In many cases it would be found that the need would be sufficiently met by the provision of well-defined tracks:' (Addison, 1931)

One member of the Addison Committee, Mr Arthur Stretton Gaye, even felt this proposal went too far. However, to a large extent the Committee was, in coming to its opposition to open access, not assisted by any vital evidence to make the case for such access. The people who gave evidence either were not of the ramblers' ilk or they simply shied away from presenting any cogent case for access; even the evidence presented by the nascent Ramblers' (Southern) Federation was particularly shallow in this respect.

Following from the seminal Dower Report of 1945 on establishing National Parks a 'Report of the National Parks Committee' chaired by Arthur Hobhouse was published in 1947. This Report strongly underlined the case made by Dower for a greater freedom of access to open countryside. Hobhouse reports:

'.for the second requirement, a progressive policy of park management will be needed, to make use of the resources of the National Parks for popular enjoyment and open-air recreation. Such a policy must be wisely applied to ensure that the peace and beauty of the countryside, and the rightful interests of the resident population, are not menaced by an excessive concentration of visitors, or disturbed by incongruous pursuits.' (38) They note *'The simplest,*

cheapest and in many respects the healthiest way of enjoying a National Park will be the way of the rambler, and all possible facilities must be provided for his accommodation and convenience. The most important of these will be well spaced and ample accommodation, free access to mountain and moorland and plenty of footpaths through the more cultivated areas.' (Hobhouse, 1947)

The Hobhouse Committee had been requested by government to go further into examining access issues than had been considered by Dower and to include the issues of access outside National Park areas. Part of their Report is therefore more generic but still pertinent to National Parks. In paragraph 290 we find:

The freedom to wander over mountain, moorland, rough grazing and other uncultivated land will be of the utmost importance to the enjoyment of National Parks. The extent of potential 'Access Land' was therefore an important factor in our selection of areas...of the proposed National Parks. 291. The freedom to wander at will is already enjoyed by the public over a large proportion of the mountain, moorland and uncultivated land in the National Park areas, but generally it is enjoyed only by tacit permission of the owners and occupiers, not as a legal right. We consider that in National Parks, public access as of right should be established over all suitable land, such as mountain, moor, heath, down, cliff and common land and uncultivated land generally, but not on land where public access would seriously conflict with other essential uses.' (Hobhouse, 1947)

It was not until the Countryside and Rights of Way Act 2000 that a right was given that went some way to meet this proposal. With an inconsistent mapping process following the 2000 Act, quiet countrygoers did not receive all the access which they expected and for which they should have been entitled. It is still worthy of note that only a variable but low proportion of National Parks are open to access on foot. Some fine areas of landscape features, sites of interest to naturalists or to those interested in historic landscape features are still denied appropriate access. (see note 1: p78)

In introducing the 1949 Bill to the House of Commons the Minister of Town and Country Planning, Rt. Hon. Lewis Silkin, stresses the access gains which, alas proved illusory:

It is perhaps a reason for our country's greatness that in a difficult period like the present we are not afraid to set aside time and energy for the practical measures needed to help people enjoy these beautiful areas. No one would wish to disagree with the wisdom of doing so, because the enjoyment of our leisure in the open air and the ability to leave our towns and walk on the moors and the dales without fear of interruption are, ..., just as much part of positive health and wellbeing as are the building of hospitals or insurance against sickness. I am particularly proud to introduce this Bill because it represents something which men and women have struggled for, often with little hope of success.'
(Hansard, 31 March 1949)

For the opposition, former minister, Rt. Hon. W.S. Morrison replied *"I need hardly say that I welcome this Bill. We all rejoice in anything which will make an understanding of the countryside a more general possession of our people.'* (Hansard, 31 March, 1949) So National Parks and countryside access had wide post-war support.

The Chancellor of the Exchequer, Hugh Dalton, had earlier announced he was earmarking £50 million to enable the implementation of the National Park legislation which was promised. He offers:

'It appeared to me it would be advantageous when this legislation comes along ... that there should be what I might describe as a nest egg, set aside, which could be used to

finance some of the operations necessary in order to give to the public permanent access to the National Parks. I do not contemplate that this £50, 000, 000 will all be spent at once. It would be spent over a period of four or five years and it would be possible to replenish the fund if it were exhausted.'
(Hansard, 10 April, 1946)

If this money actually had been available then many long-running issues could have been resolved at an early date.

Ramblers recognition of the landscape value of National Parks

When Sir Charles Trevelyan was making a speech about the growth of the rambling movement, he was reported as making the link between the demand for the opening up of areas for walking and the need for preservation through National Parks with *'Solitude and quietude was necessary as civilisation to mankind.'* (Manchester Federation of Ramblers', 1930) Trevelyan was speaking to the 1929 CPRE National Countryside Conference held in Manchester prior to moving north to continue with a conference on the 'Lake District as a National Park.' This later stage was chaired by a Mr C. Roberts, a member of the Cumbrian Regional Planning Scheme, who in supporting National Parks *'did not wish the Lake District turned into a popular rural Blackpool.'* Lord Ullswater's letter, read to conference, notes *'Let us endeavour to keep the countryside as country for recreation, rest, and enjoyment of the busy townsfolk in search of change and holiday.'* The reporter of that conference noted that few dissented from Professor Abercrombie's view *'that Lake District roads should not be widened or straightened if only to prevent their use as speedways and the inevitable consequent commercialisation.'* (Manchester, Federation of Ramblers', 1930) The key point is the ramblers were co-operating with the wider amenity movement and there was an increasing recognition of the common cause between the two strands of the movement. Stephenson went so far as to state *'The idea of protecting natural beauty and then prohibiting public enjoyment of it is preposterous and impracticable.'* (Stephenson, 1989)

Cyril Joad argues for Nature and access as a basis for designating National Parks:

'that the purpose of National Parks was to establish retreats in which men "could enjoy Nature and the solitude broken only by the companionship of wild things". For my part, I would wish to have it so broken. Nature is withholding something of her full powers to charm and to stimulate, unless she vouchsafes you a glimpse of a few small animals on your walk. I spoke of the effect of spiritual blankness and impoverishment produced by the publicly-owned properties of the National Trust. No small part of this effect is, I think, due to the almost complete absence of wild life to attract the attention and stimulate the interest of the walker, and, if his heart is in the right place, to gladden it. ...I should myself, then, adduce as an additional argument for National Parks that, by providing a sanctuary for wild things, they would assure to the walker in perpetuity the joy of savouring the full richness of nature. In adducing this argument I am, of course, assuming and endorsing the instinctive belief of the normal human being that animals are in the world not for their own sake but for his.' (Joad, n.d.)

Despite Joad's misguided view of the relationship between people and Nature, there remains the basic tenet of the need for people to experience wild places in areas where the protection afforded to those areas is of the highest status. Joad did qualify this position when he notes he was in agreement:

'with Dr. Vaughan Cornish that an adequate environment for "the English people must include landscapes into which one can retire and entirely lose sight of man and his works." Grant again that, as I suggested previously, what is involved

is a scale of comparative values, and that on this scale the well-being of citizens, not physical well-being only but spiritual, should come first, and you will grant, too, the walkers' plea that, before it is too late, areas of England should be set aside where an environment of unspoilt wild Nature can be assured.' (Joad, n.d.)

Cyril Joad reiterates his thesis *'Secondly, before it is too late, certain areas of England must be set aside as nature reserves, where men may be assured of occasional solitude, of the refreshment of country sights and sounds and of the companionship of wild things.'* (Joad, 1937) There is a subtle change of tone in respect of wild landscapes becoming nature reserves but we should not read too much into words we currently use a little differently but with a greater clarity of understanding than when they were used in the 1930s. The interactions between people, wildlife and nature reserves, and open landscapes is still very much an area where different factions come to very differing conclusions

Clough Williams-Ellis shares the highest aims for the human spirit:

'Well, it is the physical and spiritual need (still largely unconscious and unrealised) of these herded millions, divorced from the land yet lacking all the urbanity of a full and civilised city life, that justifies the demand of National Parks, for I perceive, as I have already confessed, that only public enjoyment can justify great efforts for the preservation of beauty – whether the thing in question be a masterpiece by man or God. The best things that are still left to us must now clearly be guarded not from the people but for them, else democracy is a farce and education and added leisure a heartless mockery. We are all now apprehensively aware that a mere handful of active speculators of only average barbarity can quite easily and irreparably destroy the virginity of a whole territory in no more than a year or two with their paltry impertinences, so that even outlandish

but lovely places that we had believed everlastingly impregnable are vulgarised almost overnight, their magic driven clean away for generations to come, perhaps for ever.

Yet some of us still have an obstinate faith in the ultimate return of civic sanity, a general normal healthy sensibility to natural beauty without our present unhappy itch to maul, exploit, and mishandle it. We want impregnable strongholds of natural beauty utterly free from any possible act or threat of sacrilegious barbarity for ever – oases of loveliness from which, one day, we may sally forth and reconquer the surrounding wilderness.' (Williams-Ellis, 1937)

Not only the preservationist argument but the establishment of the fundamental relationship between people and Nature were sought. This is reflected in Solnit's conclusion *'rural walking has found a moral imperative in the love of nature that has allowed it to defend and open up the countryside.'* (Solnit, 2001)

Patrick Abercrombie and Sydney Kelly comment on the potential conflict between the purposes of National Parks:

'To over-emphasise the scenery and flora-fauna aspect would defeat the whole object of the human use of these glorious open spaces; while, on the contrary, to allow them to be overrun or exploited, and especially to cater for a type of amusement which might be just as easily be satisfied in less beautiful surroundings, would be equally to destroy the first two objects.' (Abercrombie & Kelly, 1932)

Nan Fairbrother some years after the designation of National Parks, held a very negative view and regarded potential conflict as a major problem *'The problem of people in the Parks arises from the two chief difficulties: that there are too many of us, and that we come for different and often incompatible types of recreation.'* (Fairbrother, 1970) If the vision objective for quiet, appropriate recreation in our

National Parks is remembered and used as a guiding principle then the nature and scale of any potential problem should rapidly diminish.

In the early 1930s the Ramblers' and other outdoor recreation bodies joined with some of the leading national conservation bodies to issue ***An Appeal to Ramblers, Cyclists, Campers, Hostellers, and all who love the Beauty of Britain*** **to join the campaign for national parks, an appeal which starts with the words *'We all love the British countryside*.** (Anon, n.d.) This coming together of disparate organisations for common cause was triggered by the Addision Report, and the lack of subsequent government action during the years of the depression brought a more sharply focused campaign for National Parks to the fore. It was in such a context that organisations such as the Friends of the Lake District and the Standing Council for National Parks came into existence and successfully prosecuted the case leading to the National Parks and Access to the Countryside Act of 1949, and encompassing the two primary objectives.

Underlying the Ramblers' case for National Parks and access to them lie not just the physical exercise nor the health related benefits - important as these are in themselves. There is a full recognition that exploring areas of fine landscapes can give rise to health, to inspiration, to stimulus for creativity and can add a spiritual dimension, a recognition also that humanity is but a small part of Nature and that our places lie within Nature. The human need for wilder, more natural and tranquil places, is a basic element in our humanity. Herein lie matters that we are too often reluctant to articulate today and, potentially as the pressures on society change but increase, may lie a relevant future agenda.

Spiritual values

Charles Trevelyan believes:

> *'And it is not only a question of physical exercise only, it is also a question of spiritual values. Without vision the people perish and without sight of the beauty of Nature the spiritual power of the British people will be atrophied. The longing, too often thwarted longing, for natural beauty and the great unspoiled spaces is a most touching and hopeful thing in the modern city population. The condition of any real value in modern city life is holidays spent in the country.'* Trevelyan continues *'And it makes this provision of National Parks increasingly and urgently necessary. By the side of religion, by the side of science, by the side of poetry and art, stands natural beauty, not as a rival to these, but as the common inspirer and nourisher of them all, and with a secret of her own besides.'* (CPRE, 1937)

John Dower notes *'Professor Trevelyan has given so clear and admirable an exposition of the essential purpose of National Parks – and of the spiritual vision which lies behind that purpose -'*.(CPRE, 1937) The thread of preservation of fine scenery for the physical and spiritual needs of the whole nation is thus the fundamental purpose that underlies their designation, a purpose equally valid in the twenty-first century.

Kenneth Spence, after referring to the potential conflict between the protection of quietude and the increasing use of National Parks for quiet recreation by larger numbers of walkers, notes there is little danger of losing *'...something of the highest spiritual value.'* (Spence, 1937) within those dedicated areas. This is an issue we have always had, and will continue to grapple with, but this is a matter with which the English feel most uncomfortable and rarely like to air in public. Yet, to a significant extent, the understanding of such issues in the context of our relationship with Nature holds many keys for the future well-being of our society.

Figure 11: Tarr Steps, Exmoor National Park

Figure 12: Tom Stephenson

Note 1: A comparison of public open land:
National Park access land figures from Natural England post CRoW mapping. This only includes land mapped under s4 of CRoW. It will be noted a few A.O.N.Bs have a higher proportion of access land than National Parks despite their not having the second statutory purpose. The North Pennines (68%), Nidderdale (41%), and the Forest of Bowland (34 %) being the highest figures.

National Park Name	Total Area National Park (Ha)	Area Open Access (Ha)	% NP Open access
DARTMOOR	95575	46671	49%
EXMOOR	69312	17607	25%
LAKE DISTRICT	229377	114547	50%
NEW FOREST	56652	17236	30%
NORTH YORK MOORS	144106	47976	33%
NORTHUMBERLAND	105093	60314	57%
PEAK DISTRICT	143783	53930	38%
SOUTH DOWNS	165269	8271	5%
THE BROADS	30151	148	0%
YORKSHIRE DALES	176793	109977	62%
Total	**1216113**	**476675**	**39%**

Chapter 3 - The Landscape Vision for National Parks

'...I love the English country which I think the most beautiful in the world, feel intensely patriotic in regard to it, and care passionately that it should be defended and preserved. Like all lovers of good things, I want others to love it too,' (Joad, 1946)

'...preserving and enhancing their natural beauty...' (National Parks Act, 1949)

'...to conserve and enhance the natural beauty, wildlife and cultural heritage..' (Environment Act, 1995)

Designation of National Parks *'...may... take into account its wildlife and cultural heritage,'* (Natural England and Rural Communities Act, 2006)

'...the bridge between our aesthetic sensibilities and the practical politics of conservation.' (Phillips, 1985)

The campaign for the protection of beautiful landscapes was frequently regarded as the role of the middle class 'Romantics' – the intelligentsia, the artists, the people of 'taste' – people who paid paternalistic regard to the needs of the workers in the cities to re-create in the expected nationally protected areas. Recreational organisations were, as we saw in Chapter 2, also fierce advocates of the protection of fine landscapes. A number of outdoor recreational organisations came together in the 1930's to campaign for the protection of the special qualities in National Park areas along with enhanced access and the right to roam in such landscapes and in the wider countryside. Their manifesto includes:

'We all love the British countryside. We desire that its beauty should everywhere be kept unspoilt. But certain stretches of country – mountain and moorland, forest and heath, downland and rugged coastline – are distinguished by a richer and wilder beauty, and by freedom from close cultivation which gives – or should give – a corresponding freedom to wander at will. For these stretches we have a special love and a more intense desire that their loveliness should be kept not only unspoilt but unaltered, that their freedom should be not only maintained but made complete and irrevocable. These stretches, if we but turn our desires into sufficient determined and united actions, are the future National Parks of Britain." They add *"Everywhere, even in the wildest places, there is some sort of use and occupation of land and the possibility of change and disfigurement! A few ugly houses in a secluded valley head, a petrol station on a moorland road, a quarry tip or a pylon line on a mountain side, may destroy the harmonious beauty of many square miles of landscape.'* Put simply *'To love a place is to wish it to survive unspoiled.'* (SCNP, 1938)

George Trevelyan argues that the call for National Parks was increasingly mounted because of the rapid loss of places of valued natural beauty:

'Two things are characteristic of our age, and more particularly of our island. The conscious appreciation of natural beauty, and the rapidity with which it is being destroyed. No doubt it is partly because the destruction is so rapid that the appreciation is so loud.' He is clear such a love of beauty is long established in the English psyche *'it is quite possible that our ancestors were as fond of natural beauty as we are, but they talked about it less often and less elaborately about it.'* (Trevelyan, 1931)

Clough Williams-Ellis recognises that in the protection of fine landscapes, whilst hugely desirable in itself, there was a need to ensure that the whole population understood and supported the case for preservation:

'But in order that the very heritage itself may be spared, and shall not dissolve utterly away at this unaccustomed touch, this overdue presentation must be assuredly be made, for it is altogether too dangerous that the vast majority of its heirs should be insensitive to the intrinsic loveliness, ignorant of its pleasure-giving potentialities or its historical value, that they should still be without pride in its possession and careless in its preservation. To ensure that at any rate our chief national treasures, both of landscape and architecture, shall survive these difficult transitional times, that they may give pride and pleasure to our possibly more civilised successors, they must now attract to themselves a general popularity and appreciation – a wide democratic good will, that will protect them from injury and maintain their integrity when the traditional guardians are perhaps no longer able to defend them.' (Williams-Ellis, 1937)

Protection from development

In a simplistic way, the vision for the protection of England's finest landscapes was based on the rate of change to the rural fabric and to agriculture largely through the spread of urban developments, which began after the Great War. F.R. Sandbach describes this:

'After the First World War there was mounting concern about preserving the countryside in the face of virtually unplanned urban growth and ribbon development, an accelerated growth of electricity generation with its associated amenity problems of pylons and overhead wires, afforestation, skywriting and caravan encampments. ...During the inter-war period various aspects of preservation warranted special attention from the voluntary amenity movement; of these the campaign to obtain National Parks was one of the most significant.' (Sandbach, 1978)

This summarises the preservation position succinctly and confirmed the views, evident from the early nineteenth century, of the 'rash assault' being made on the finest landscapes. However, such a view misses the significance of the pioneers' vision as to the positive aspects of protecting landscapes, an aspect we too often ignore today and goes towards explaining why the National Park movement is too often on the defensive.

Despite the dark days of the Great War, a Sheffield rambler, Charles Chandler, feels strongly about the English countryside *'We have had – and still have – one of the most beautiful countries in the world. But we have never troubled as a nation about keeping it beautiful. The commercial spirit which gets into our very blood as soon as the town fixes its grip upon us drives all the sentiment out of man.'* (quoted in Taylor, 1997)

The 1929 CPRE Countryside Conference noted a range of factors regarded as disfiguring the countryside, in the words of CPRE president, Lord Crawford, to *'a grievous extent.'* (Manchester Federation of Ramblers', 1930) The list would not be out of place on our current agendas: uncontrolled or poorly controlled development, inharmonious building, unsightly roads, overhead power transmission, outdoor advertisements, ill-designed petrol filling stations, litter, refuse dumps etc. Patrick Abercrombie and Sydney Kelly express concern about road developments in the Lake District and recommend *'The roads therefore within Lakeland or the National Park Area of this regional scheme are to be designed and maintained for local traffic and for national purposes only so far as they serve as a national object in the Area.'* They add Lakeland is *'not a speed track area.'* (Abercrombie & Kelly, 1932) Robert Mattocks was more taciturn in his approach to development in the Lake District *'When we come to…definite proposals and suggestions we are much assisted by Nature. In so much of our area building and road making are impossible owing to the nature of the ground...'* (Mattocks, 1930) However, his view did not stand in the face of the determined developer. Inherent is recognition that some development might occur but that its nature and scale had to be considered if it was to be accommodated within the landscape. Trevelyan notes the threats:

> *'Every month beautiful properties, threatened by the march of bricks and mortar, or by other profanation, are offered to it [i.e. National Trust].'* He continues *'In an age when beauty, especially beauty of nature and landscape, is being destroyed with unexampled rapidity by modern inventions and economic and residential developments, the desire to save beloved places from the ruin is much more widely and intensely felt than ever before.'* He notes *'The State, whether rightly or wrongly, declines to hold land for this purpose.'* (Trevelyan, 1929)

Yet Cyril Joad warns, despite what he would have regarded as a partial surrender by Abercrombie and Kelly, we should *'Once recognize that motoring has created a new situation and that in relation to the motor's capacity for ubiquitous penetration. England is too small for any solitude to remain solitary, unless it is deliberately protected, and you become a supporter of the case of National Parks at any cost.'* (Joad, n.d.) Joad, potentially at odds with Trevelyan in a fundamental belief, however takes the presence of rural 'shacks' as an indicator *'That the English by and large have little or no sense of beauty or that, if they have, they allow the utterance of its still, small voice to be smothered by the blare of advertisers or the cries of profit makers ... [who] ...have done their best to make it mean and ugly.'* (Joad, 1946)

One of the problems of the 1930s and early 1940s was the hold landowners had over potential restrictions on the use of their land. In many cases, a restriction on a landowner's right of development would result in compensation being paid by local authorities and, as many highly valued landscapes were in rural areas with consequent low rateable values and local authorities' low budgets, the political will and the ability to restrict undesirable development was severely curtailed. Sir Charles Trevelyan recognises that budgets, even then seen as very limited, for National Park purposes would entail *'Much of this money would no doubt go to compensation of landowners whose rights of development would be restricted in order to secure the amenity of the regions turned into National Parks.'* (CPRE, 1937)

Arthur Dower, responding to Trevelyan notes:

'Without compensation it is impossible under the Act to restrict building to any adequate extent. But building is not the only or the most serious threat, and nearly all the other dangers – mining and quarrying, large-scale afforestation, water-catchment and water-power schemes, overhead cable lines, road development, noise – fall entirely outside the control of planning authorities.' (CPRE, 1937)

Luckily more enlightened planning legislation followed, the Planning Act of 1947, but was unfortunately timed before the 1949 Act, which was to change this unhelpful system in offering better planning protection although it never fully offered the degree of protection National Park areas would require.

John Dower, in discussing the extent of potential National Parks, is clear that robust planning alone will not be an adequate tool to manage such designated landscapes:

'I mean the preservation of the beauty, the openness and the agricultural usefulness of all the countryside of England. I have particularly in mind that part of the country classed as 'upland hill' - the great reservoir of mountains and moors and rougher grasslands out of which National Parks must be chosen.' He adds *'I would estimate that potential National Park area of Great Britain at something like a quarter of the*

whole country, 22,000 square miles. We need a policy for the conservation of the whole of this area. There is none too much of it.' (CPRE 1937)

Dower had exposed both the strength and weakness of the National Park argument – protecting limited areas so designated might threaten more unacceptable change in the remainder of the countryside. National Park pioneer Kenneth Spence raised this issue at the CPRE conference and the chairman, Sir Gwilym Gibbon, addresses the matter in his closing summary *'If the two were in any way incompatible, to my mind the preservation of the general countryside was of more importance than the special areas of National Parks. But the two are not incompatible; they are in fact complementary and concentration on National Parks should not lessen our efforts for the general countryside.'* (CPRE, 1937) Whilst CPRE was a significant player in establishing National Parks, their operation today still focuses on the wider countryside.

John Dower entered the quagmire in the debate as to the major issues - which extensive areas should be designated. There was little outright opposition to the need for such designations, and indeed after World War II the arguments were more towards which areas should be designated, an issue still live today, and whether, in 1949, the local councils should have their recently awarded planning powers and other controls handed over to independent National Park bodies. If the National Parks were to be for the nation then they were to help resolve the dilemma Antoine de Saint-Euxpéry notes, in a different context, that protecting fine landscapes where otherwise *'...innumerable assaults which every society necessarily makes upon the liberty of the individual...'* (de Saint-Euxpéry, 1961) might be resolved in favour of the Nation and the future. What Jean-Paul Sartre might, taking a literary liberty, describe the priority for National Parks as *'Our aim is precisely to establish the human kingdom as a pattern of values in distinction from the material world.'* (Sartre, 1946)

The National Park movement did not promote a total restriction on new development; some accommodation especially for youth hostels, for example, was readily recommended before the legislation came in 1949. Yet Trevelyan says, after recognising that land management would still be in the hands of landowners, *'It is not change, but preservation of the existing state of things that is mainly aimed at.'* (CPRE, 1937). The reference was intended to convey the wider protection of the farmed landscape but Trevelyan was little able to foresee the changes in farming practice that would emerge particularly after the end of World War II. However, like the main campaign for landscape protection, led by The Standing Committee for National Parks, Friends of the Lake District, the Council for the Preservation of Rural England and their ilk, the amenity organisations were not against change. National Parks were not to be preserved like a jam but the rate, nature and scale of change had to be controlled in the national interest. The coalition of amenity groups note, in their 1930's pamphlet:

> *'Where a limited amount of new building is permitted, style and materials must be strictly controlled to harmonise with the landscape and with the existing buildings; ...though building which is sound and harmonious should not, in general, be appreciably more expensive than that which is ugly and discordant.'* (Anon, n.d.)

Despite this basic principle too many of those who find National Parks irksome to their material aspirations still try and argue that conservation is about "preservation in aspic". People who use such arguments have no substantive case to promote.

Public interest in planning was, prior to 1949, largely restricted to significant issues, for example ribbon development, major roads, overhead power lines, quarries. The chairman of the 1937 CPRE conference, Gibbon, sums up this predicament they faced:

> *'A good deal of the difficulty in obtaining the necessary backing arose because the ordinary person was singularly lacking in imagination. The process of the attrition of amenities was a gradual one and because it was gradual it did not obtain headlines in the papers. A means of stirring the imagination of the ordinary citizen had to be found, despite this gradual process, as if these areas were being subjected to a great cataclysm, as they will be in time if attrition is allowed to continue.'* (CPRE, 1937)

Ignoring Gibbon's patronising phraseology the underlying comment of having failed to engage the widest backing for the National Park movement, other than from a few preservationists and committed ramblers, is more an issue today, not least with some who live and have chosen to live, within the boundaries of designated areas. His allusion to the loss of beauty through the process of incremental development is one, which has escaped the clutches of planners since 1947.

The coalition of amenity groups argues some specific types of development would be most unwelcome in National Park landscapes:

> *'Advertisements and petrol stations must be severely restricted. Pylons and poles must be avoided wherever possible, any necessary transmission lines being diverted or placed underground, even if this involves an increase in the initial cost. Aerodromes and landing-grounds should not be allowed within National Park areas, and all low flying should be prohibited.'* They add '*A very strict control over highway improvements is of vital importance. Through motor traffic should be discouraged, and motor touring should be confined to the existing road system,'* (Anon, n.d.)

The debate about who should control development in National Parks is still a very live issue and currently a significant element of the political ambition of the Liberal Democrat party is to have such a service democratically controlled. They do not regard National Park authorities as so qualifying. The newest member of the National Park family, the South Downs, deals only with major planning applications whilst the established local authorities handle the smaller, often more domestic matters. However, such local decisions are largely handled by officers alone and do not involve council member consideration. The National Park authority will have to monitor such a scheme to ensure that areas of the designated landscape are not affected by incremental and local decision-making.

At another level, two National Parks are experimenting with the direct election of members to the South Downs and Peak District National Park authorities. These experiments will be watched with interest - in some cases hope, in others apprehension. How far such a scheme could go to ensure the designated landscapes remain national and allow for the settling of some local political unrest will be monitored carefully by all concerned.

Control over development is one of the few powers exercisable by National Park authorities. Creative schemes for enhancing the landscape depend on the strength of the membership, the strength of vision and direction, and the staffing of the authorities. Thus exercising a negative control has not only been the most contested of duties, where many local authorities would like to claim the powers away from the National Park authorities, but it gives rise to local perceptions of distrust when these have been carried out in the name of the nation. Nonetheless, despite widespread examples of poor planning decisions to allow development against advice and policy, development control has been an effective tool in meeting the vision for National Parks.

Harvey Taylor sees the need to protect landscapes and the more recent movement towards lifestyles more in harmony with the natural environment as *'Although the underlying urge was reformist, romantic impulses cannot be discounted in the wider challenge to growing commercialisation and the continuing prevalence of utilitarian values.'* (Taylor, 1997) Whatever the current urge and driving force the need to protect fine countryside from those people with different values continues to be a major battleground in England significantly, but far from particularly, in National Parks.

Protection of landscapes for re-creation

The Council for the Preservation of Rural England (CPRE) National Countryside Conference in 1929 held a discussion on National Parks led by Lord Bledisloe. Bledisloe comments *'if there was an insistent need for such parks in countries of vast areas and small populations, surely more overwhelming is the necessity in a small country like ours.'* The relationship to the needs of the population to enjoy such protected landscapes was a foundation of our National Parks. Vaughan Cornish adds they should be a *'pedestrians' paradise and not opened up for motor roads or organised recreation.'* (Federation of Manchester Ramblers', 1930)

The Chairman of the Lake District session of the conference, Charles Roberts, comments *'he did not wish the Lake District turned into a popular rural Blackpool.'* Lord Ullswater adds *'let us endeavour to keep the countryside as country for the recreation, rest, and enjoyment of the busy towns-folk in search of change and holiday.'* Sir Charles Trevelyan argues *'England had greater need of a National Park than any other country. Solitude and quietude was as necessary as civilisation to mankind.'* (Federation of Manchester Ramblers', 1930). Thus, the protectors of landscape saw the value to humanity of achieving National Parks as a necessary concomitant to the value of protecting fine landscapes "for their own sake".

Vaughan Cornish counters Dower's demand that National Parks were only for mountain and moorland areas *'Our first demand is that the scheme of National Parks for England should provide at least one example of each principle type of scenery which still remains in its wild, open and natural state.'* (CPRE, 1937) Abercrombie and Kelly note *'in a National Park it may be essential definitely to limit development for the sake of the major object – the national enjoyment of wild scenery and country.'* (Abercrombie & Kelly, 1932) Earlier Mattocks, writing about the southern Lake District believes *'one of the finest scenery in England lies within the boundary of the Region, and it is a national asset of such value that it demands careful preservation by those in whose hands its fate lies.'* (Mattocks, 1930)

Arthur Gardner provides us with an example of landscape change and protection felt to be necessary for National Parks. *'The New Forest…is already a possession of the Crown, and all we have to beware of is the Forestry Commission, in whose charge it is, does not destroy its wilder and more natural woods in its infatuation for the dull monotony of conifer plantations which seem the staple of commercial forestry.'* (Gardener, 1942). The supporters of landscape protection demanded that the 'English natural' rather than an alien character for our landscapes should be preserved.

The coalition of amenity organisations pamphlet notes *'the detailed elements that compose the natural beauty must be carefully protected – the woodlands, the roadside trees, the hedgerows, the wild flowers and ferns and the bird and animal life.'* (Standing Committee for National Parks, 1938) People realised, as Ananitchev writes *'nature was no longer just a static background, but a reliable and trustful friend vulnerable to betrayal.'* (Council for Europe, 2004) Indeed the protection of landscape movement, it can be readily argued, is seeking landscape change through the enhancement of the recognised special qualities of the area, by reversing as in the case of commercial forestry, change that was deemed unsuitable and unacceptable. Whilst enhancement formed a major part of the wording of the first statutory purpose of National Parks and of areas of outstanding natural beauty it has been the element, which we have been least successful in achieving.

R.G. Stapledon notes:

> *'A national park must not be rendered hideous or unbeautiful. Everything must be done with discretion, usefulness and beauty being of equal importance. Usefulness and beauty have never been incompatible relative to anything that man can achieve – it is only laziness and greed that have been responsible for all the ugliness we now have to suffer.'* He adds *'My conception of National Parks for Britain is therefore large blocks of country kept beautiful ...where the maximum number of people can find pleasure and do things without being herded together – food and timber, let me emphasize, should be produced within the confines of a National Park.'* (Stapledon, 1937)

Today we would read tensions between Stapledon's arguments and his conclusion, not least regarding the amount of commercial coniferisation (or afforestation) within the boundaries of designated areas and regarding how far society is willing to contribute to the cultural agricultural landscape. The great naivety of the belief woodland (aka forestry) and agricultural developments continuing in traditional ways as being sufficient to protect the landscape character, of not needing to influence their processes is still, to the detriment of many designated landscapes, too prevalent a current view. The question of what public benefits from significant amounts of governmental grants to rural industries remains a topical question.

Beauty for its own sake

Kenneth Spence was an early and largely unsung hero of the campaign for National Parks (see Cousins, 2009) and he clearly believed in the compatibility of the twin purpose approach of preservation of landscape and quiet recreation. He argues:

'Perhaps it will be thought here that I am begging the question as to what is the real protection that should be extended to the wilds and solitudes of our mountain lands. If I would restrict the motorist, wink at the pass-storming cyclist and encourage the walker, am I not being illogical, and is not the only preservation of these places one that will exclude to all intents and purposes mankind at large? ...My answer, and one to which I believe many would subscribe, is that in Great Britain there exist (though unequally distributed) enough lovely uncultivated moorlands and mountains which, if all were thrown open for public access, would, except near the big centres of population, still remain in essence the wilds and solitudes they are now.' (Spence, 1937)

Increasingly today we, I believe, better understand the relationship between landscape, habitat and wildlife, and cultural heritage and, to some limited degree, the participants are beginning to explore each other's agenda. Yet in the pre- and immediate post-World War II years, the idea of protecting areas for a range of preservation needs was poorly developed. Those whose primary interest was in nature conservation somehow regarded as different (and less precious) the beauty of landscape. The Flora's League representative at the CPRE 1937 Conference notes *'In a broad sense National Parks and nature reserves were not compatible. They were compatible up to a point, in that you might have a nature reserve within a National Park. Even then they would have to surround it with a barbed wire fence and defend the wild flowers.'* (CPRE, 1937). The underlying line of thinking by which, to a significant degree, nature and landscape protection were entirely separate matters, was enshrined in the National Parks and Access to the Countryside Act, 1949 and has started to be partially corrected with the principle behind the formation of Natural England in 2006.

It is a great loss that for many decades we have had this sometimes-uneasy twin approach to the totality of landscape protection. There were voices that did recognise the fallacy of the position taken eventually in 1949. The Secretary of the Society for the Promotion of Nature Reserves argues, *'There were two aspects of the National Parks question, one recreational and the other nature reserves. The recreational point of view was mostly present at that morning meeting, but it was the reserve of the flora and fauna which made a park. He hoped that this question would not be forgotten.'* (CPRE, 1937). It was not forgotten but disregarded.

Nan Fairbrother, despite the general support for re-constructing landscapes, recognises *'our heaths and downs and moors seem natural to us, and maintenance should aim to keep them so.'* (Fairbrother, 1970) Early, in a reference to designated landscapes, she notes *'fine scenery is precious because it is beautiful: its beauty has a price we are willing to pay by giving up unsuitable land-uses and by grants of money if needed.'* (Fairbrother, 1970) This judgement of Fairbrother was more direct than the political consideration of the issues by Abercrombie and Kelly:

> *'The economic use of wild country, generally so rich in minerals, at once comes into conflict with scenic preservation. It requires a most careful and broadminded study in order to determine in certain areas which is in the real national interest, namely to exploit a certain mineral or stone in the national interest or to preserve untouched a certain piece of scenery or object of historical interest. At present the first is almost invariably given an overriding importance, which has to be upset very often at great*

expense; but the best interests of the country may possibly be served by obtaining the same product elsewhere.'
(Abercrombie & Kelly, 1932)

What was touched upon here was a recognition that unless there was an unanswerable national need then the extractive industries should not be allowed to operate in National Parks - once an important element of government planning policies for National Parks but not for areas of outstanding natural beauty.

Long term stewardship

The founding of the Friends of the Lake District in 1934 was a huge catalyst in the movement to campaign for National Parks. The formation meeting was held in Keswick, where Sir Charles Trevelyan asks *'How can we avoid having periodically to call on the efforts of people of goodwill locally and nationally to save the chief values of the Lake District? How can we put this great treasure of scenery, wildness and natural beauty beyond the reach of thoughtless destruction and unenlightened impairment?'* Trevelyan listed some ongoing threats to the landscape from mineral deposit working, ribbon development, housing in the valleys, to new hotels and motor parks before adding with rousing intensity *'There should be no delay; lost wildness could never be recovered, beauty once destroyed could only slowly be recreated. Lakeland was irreplaceable. Determine to leave it your successors as great a glory as it is to you.'* (Friends of the Lake District internal files) Despite some knowledge of what were regarded as special qualities, it is the enduring legacy to be left for future generations which underlines National Park status, which is a crucial point. The hint of what we call sustainability, of leaving the unimpaired beauty for future generations, becomes the important concept for long-term stewardship of our National Parks.

Sustainability is a current "buzzword" but few understand what it means and few question what the implications of adopting such a concept imply. The most vociferous opponents of landscape protection call it the "hair shirt" approach. It is argued here that if we had adopted more intensely the visions of the National Park founders then our National Parks would be leaders in showing what sustainable landscapes with wildlife and sustainable communities can offer for the country as a whole. Maybe re-visiting their vision will enable us to come to grips with the worthiness of the sustainability agenda.

Figure 13: Cader Idris, Snowdonia National Park

Chapter 4: Whither National Parks? Unfinished Business - can we develop an ethic and vision for National Parks?

'The creator seeks fellow-creators, those, who inscribe new values on new tables.' (Nietzsche, 1892)

'I believe in the primacy of man above the individual and the universal above the particular.' (de Saint-Euxpéry, 1942)

England now has a family of ten National Parks (along with the areas of outstanding natural beauty and their counterparts in Wales) and a debate has started as to their value, role and function. This is an important debate not just for the heirs of the designation movement but also for the well-being of the people of the country, and of their future quality of life. Hard questions will be posed and need thoughtful answers. The debate is nationally political, local in areas with National Parks, and within the family of National Parks. However, whilst these remain separate debates there is little, other than the government review of governance of National Parks, to suggest that the critical mass for a full national debate has yet been reached. It is simmering beneath the surface as a volcano unsure when it will break out. In the meantime, the media is rarely without a story, especially local, to designated areas. Only major issues, such as the proposed high speed railway through the Chilterns AONB, have brought a wider public debate about the value of designated areas in recent times.

Today there are few people alive who recall the campaign for National Parks and decreasing in number are those who sat at the feet of the pioneers. We have a new generation to address. Indeed, as the assault on the integrity of National Parks becomes more intense it leads to greater friction with those with an interest in the designated areas. The conservation, economic and social pressure groups forget their interrelationship of a shared purpose – what we now brand as sustainability. Increasing demands for more unsustainable economic development ignore the price of selling out the basic human need of treasured landscapes. This is not new; it is just a more rapid and intense process than the founders recognised. We have again forgotten that our social, creative and economic health depends *a priori* on the quality of and access to the landscape in which we live. The defenders of beauty and human values are put increasingly on the defensive and the developer, when losing the argument, uses the bitter rhetoric 'conservationists prefer landscapes to people.' J. Passmore poses the jibe *'It might well seem odd that the conservationist-...-is so confident that he knows how to save posterity when he cannot save his own contemporaries.'* (Passmore, 1974) Other writers with a conservationist leaning, such as Charlie Pye-Smith and Chris Hall, make explicit the dilemma *'...conservationists have sometimes been as guilty of selfishness and elitism as the landowners they attack. We must establish not just why we conserve nature, but for whom.'* (Pye-Smith & Hall, 1987)

One of the easiest tasks for those who doubt the ability of the system of designated landscapes to protect those areas is to tour around them and, with the utmost simplicity, compile a list of landscape features and developments, which detract from the special qualities of these landscapes. Many National Parks have unsightly non-native plantation afforestation covering significant areas. This was a failing anticipated by, and described in, the run up to 1949. Where is the logic to controlling grey squirrels when our native reds are threatened, yet not think to defend our native oak, perhaps the most enduring symbol of being English we have in the landscape, from the onslaught of introduced species and diseases of trees? Arthur Gardner's call for what *'we have to beware of is the Forestry Commission, ..., not to destroy its wilder and more natural woods in its infatuation for the dull monotony of conifer plantations.'* (Gardener, 1942) would be found in vain. The Forestry Commission has changed, radically, since the late 1980s. We cannot, nor would we want to try, to create the original wildwood but we can bring our much less practised skills of woodmanship to allow natural processes to work with indigenous species to the benefit and enhancement of the character of our local landscapes. This might be for example, through using trees of native provenance to replace the alien plantation species. Removing the aliens need only take a short time period, but restoring the more characteristic woodlands will take centuries, and having long-term management strategies or land use planning is not what we are good at in England. The newly emerging economics of wood-fuel offer great opportunity for skilling and equipping a workforce and would be helpful to sustaining local communities.

Developments have continued despite the earlier recognition of their immediate and cumulative potential to erode seriously the quality of the landscapes. The government agency formerly responsible for the welfare of our designated areas, the Countryside Commission, noted *'The Commission regards it as vital that afforestation is in keeping with the character of the parks.'* (Countryside Commission, 1985). Yet how can any fine landscape be protected or enhanced by intrinsically fundamental, non-characteristic changes to the landscape? With this type of national support for the National Parks, is it any wonder major battles were rarely won, and confidence in the designation has been so shattered?

Part of the objective of designation was to halt and reverse unsuitable landscape changes, that were in part openly articulated by the proponents of National Parks. The Hobhouse Report records that undesirable landscape changes were occurring through agriculture, and notes *'...the loss of moorland; loss of hedgerows and the erecting of fencing; the felling of hedgerow and other timber'* (Hobhouse, 1947)

There might have been a degree of naivety in respect of general tree felling. However, Hobhouse and other contemporary commentators under-anticipated the potential damage from a number of these and other rural operations. Hobhouse was also concerned with the impact of forestry, water gathering, electricity distribution, telegraph and telephone wires, radar and radio installations, military training, aviation, roads, outdoor advertising and the provision of some types of tourist accommodation. (See Hobhouse, 1947). Much can be and should have been done about these matters if we are to demonstrate how life is still possible in our wilder landscapes without the need to adopt standards of urban 'grot' that so characterise and make uniform our major settlements. In some cases, the solution is quick and easy; in others, we have to wait much longer. Even reservoir dams have a finite life. These, and similar problems, offer the opportunity for the enhancement of designated landscapes - a word enshrined within the first statutory purpose and a word so infrequently the cause of action - and herein perhaps lies one of the greatest failures of the National Park authorities to show they are effective guardians.

To an extent, it can be shown that national agencies have worked to help the protection. The changing government support for the agricultural system has, to a small measure, helped to protect some parts of the landscape character. Such schemes are compromises and thereby undermine fundamental principles. The Countryside Commission noted the greatest challenge to our National Park landscapes *'has come from the new methods of farming.'* (Countryside Commission, 1985). This led to a small reversal of negative changes through some targeting of grants for positive, but very restricted, landscape enhancement such as rebuilding dry stone walls in limited circumstances. The age of rewarding landowners and farmers with public money for grubbing out hedgerows had then only just finished. Even current agri-environment schemes, which are starting to deliver on nature conservation enhancement pay scant regard to other designation criteria and have significantly damaged relationships between the "traditional" stewards of the farmed landscape and governmental bodies. As funding may become tighter and agricultural prices rise, it is possible that the farming community will exercise a greater independence and this may not be to the best effect of protecting a national interest.

Nature is highly regarded by residents and visitors to our designated landscapes. Yet any proposals to undertake a measure of re-wilding, to allow more natural processes, or re-introduce species which humans have made extinct are always clouded in controversy – even when the ideas have been given considerable thought prior to becoming a proposition. The removal of damaging alien species, again, for example, the grey squirrel, or fallow deer or some invasive trees and plants is resisted, showing both the inadequacy of people's understanding of, or consistent approach to, such issues but also the failure of those deeply concerned to demonstrate clearly that such matters should be in everyone's long-term interest. We can maintain a sustainable grazing system in our wilder areas. However, a basic compact between who owns the land, who farms the land, and who sets the long-term objectives for the style and intensity of grazing, and appropriate objectives for the management of that land would be a controversial process. There is no reason why some appropriate forms of land management, of our more native vegetation, walls, hedgerows, vernacular buildings, cannot be better supported. Yet the contrary, the removal of fences, not least from the clutter and barriers they form on the open common land of many of the upland fells, would need much stronger application of existing regulations. This would be more than most politicians or governmental officials can stomach. This is especially so to those who's brief and foresight are strictly parochial or time-limited by the date of the next election. Equally, we need to consider proposals for the removal of major areas of bracken or other invasive plants (especially non-native such as Himalayan Balsam) as a priority, but nobody has responsibility for action. If our National Parks are to be leaders in the sustainability debate then should they not be working towards encouraging organic farming systems? Equally, whilst we can make our National Parks wilder we cannot nor should we try to make them wildernesses. We can never recover a landscape that we do not fully understand of what they comprised or how they functioned, that is if they really existed.

Some people will say that the best protection we have had for our designated landscapes has been the power of planners to refuse planning applications. The landscapes, they say and rightly so, could have been so much more damaged if some planning applications had not been refused. Equally, it is easy to find some planning decisions, where developments have been allowed, and have destroyed the character of fine landscapes. Quarrying and mining in particular, where these have been allowed to expand hugely despite the lack of a national need, are prime examples. National necessity is too readily accepted as an economic argument for the development, often lacking rigour and remaining substantially unchallenged. So much for the value we place on designated areas. There have been some notable exceptions, for example, the work of the Dartmoor Preservation Association in helping stop the extensions to quarries for extraction of China Clay.

Figure 14: Bonehill and Grimspound, Dartmoor National Park

In most cases, we shall now have to wait until 2042 before this quarrying desecration of the landscape there, can be under consideration for ending the damage caused. Even small changes, including those allowed under the General Development Order, where small development changes or agricultural developments are excused public scrutiny, have adversely affected the landscape singly or incrementally. Hobhouse recommended a simple change and still we await its delivery. (See Hobhouse, 1947). Even the statutory undertakers, now private companies, have a degree of exemption, which brings small, often permanent damage to our finest landscapes. All such small changes may appear relatively benign in themselves but cumulatively they are, along with future potential changes, a significant threat to landscape. Hobhouse and others hoped that disfigurements to the landscape might be removed, discontinued or mitigated, but few examples of such a simple and effective method have been tried. This is usually because of significant under-funding and a lack of political will in designated areas. The current government's views on the planning system are well known and these do not auger well for the future landscapes of our designated areas.

Robert Mattocks, when he discussed a regional planning scheme for an area of land eventually designated in the southern part of the Lake District National Park, noted the planners' dilemma:

> *'in a region of this type it is not always an easy task to pick out certain areas for reservation and schedule the rest for building purposes. The whole region is full of charm that little short of its total reservation would really satisfy the enthusiast.'* Mattocks outlined his philosophy for planning in such a high amenity landscape *'In presenting the Report on Regional Planning for the Southern portion of the Lake District, the Committee are undertaking a work of an original kind. As will be seen, the District is one with a stationary population and no immediate prospect of development of an industrial nature. ...Our principal object is to keep the area as beautiful as it is now, to keep what buildings and developments may be inevitable on the right lines, and to look ahead to ensure that the existing routes for those who come to enjoy our scenery are kept safe and unspoilt,'* (Mattocks, 1930)

The antithesis, equally applied in support for National Parks, when seeking to protect their areas from undesirable developments, implied such developments should take place in undesignated landscapes. Thus, economic, social and cultural changes could occur at a more rapid pace and greater extent in the wider countryside. Yet, much of these threatened areas are equally valued, not least by local inhabitants. The question of the appropriate level of protection of undesignated areas, of areas adjacent to designated landscapes therefore arises. Does it suggest designated areas are reservoirs of countryside protection awaiting an equitable management and will eventually receive the respect and safeguards for their future enhancement?

As a number of outdoor organisations wrote in the 1930s *'A few ugly houses in a secluded valley head, a petrol station on a moorland road, a quarry tip or a pylon line on a mountain side, may destroy the harmonious beauty of many square miles of landscape.'* (Anon, n.d.) Equally Cyril Joad quotes the example of *'the blare of advertisers or the cries of the profit makers...[who]... have done their best to make it [the countryside] mean and ugly.'* (Joad, 1946)

There is no doubt stronger controls over development could put the local communities in a slightly different position from those in towns and cities and, to a more limited extent, those who live in other rural areas. Yet many people, perhaps in some places the majority of the population, have chosen to move to live within our National Parks and areas of outstanding natural beauty because of the intrinsic merits of the landscape. The more stringent controls envisaged as necessary in these designated landscapes, though not all put into place, were a basis on which the consensus for the 1949 legislation was built. The benefit of a stronger development control regime was fundamental to the vision for establishing designated areas and there were organisations and individuals who, in evidence to the Dower and Hobhouse Inquiries, stated the implication of such restrictions very openly. It is therefore strange that local communities perceive that planning guidance in National Parks is harsh, yet the evidence and the comparisons with non-designated areas suggest that the perception is more about who controls the decision making process than the policy basis for decision making.

Some vociferous local residents in designated areas want the latest technology and are prepared, in some cases, to see the high-quality landscape in which they have chosen to live degraded through the installation of communications masts or newly constructed roads for example. They want houses for local needs and blame second-home owners for pushing up house prices. Yet if the position is analysed, it is often these same people who use their properties for holiday lets, and who support significant economic development. This is even when it is often low-waged based, such as much of the tourism industry. They will never enable their employees to pay a market rate that enables them to compete in a rural housing market. The same people may have bought smallish houses, and built extensions and turned them into less-affordable housing. It is sometimes those families who make much of the need for more housing for their families who have previously sold the family house to reach the highest price achievable. However, the significant point is that serious housing need is a general rural problem and not always found to the same degree throughout our designated areas. The Standing Conference on National Parks thought it important to note *'Damage has been done to National Parks by the over-provision of houses for people living outside the Parks.'* (Standing Committee for National Parks, 1938). The earlier planning policies, having no restriction on who could purchase newly built houses, led to a significant build-up of in-migration to our National Parks. Which, whilst putting some stress on the infrastructure of such areas, were not totally a negative issue, as many of the new people brought ideas and vitality that helped sustain the communities of the designated areas.

It is the same critical residents who, in the valid search for civic pride, tend to urbanise their local landscapes. They place urban flowerbeds on roadsides, they put narcissi or even plastic daffodils, alongside the home of the wild daffodil, they erect brown signs and unauthorised advertising hoardings without any concern for visual clutter; they want more street lighting and kerbed roads. It is not just a question of taste or of good design, it is one of recognising the genius loci of where people live and celebrating those elements that contribute so much to the quality of the local landscape character and to the enjoyment of one's own community.

It is difficult to understand how we cannot replace all overhead power lines within the designated areas within the next twenty years with more supply secure underground cable supplies. In some cases, it is the combined effect of electricity generation siting and subsequent transmission and distribution causing the problem. Gerald Haythornthwaite notes what the then chairman of the Central Electricity Generating Board, Sir Christopher Hinton, had described as *'it is no use to argue that properly sited pylons and transmission lines stride grandly across the countryside. To the average man they are (consciously or un-consciously) the tentacles of industrialization creeping out into a countryside which he prefers to keep from industrialization.'* (Haythornthwaite, 1960) Greater action to remove wirescapes, much more than recent small-scale gains, which designated areas, are wisely adopting, could collectively help reduce visual intrusion and enhance landscapes. There is a cost but there are huge benefits.

Road schemes, as forecast by the founders of the National Parks in the 1930s, are still a major issue. Most National Parks have the basis of what might become a reasonable public transport system to the major areas of population. Yet it is the prevailing attitude of the majority of people who come to visit or live in the areas to want to enjoy the special qualities of the area whilst damaging it through their reluctance to avoid use of their motorcars. Changes to road character, the tarmacadaming of sparsely used rural lanes, the previous metalling of mountain passes, and the desire to park a car without consideration to its effect in the landscape are still, for many people, questions they refuse to consider in the context of the designated landscape. It would be possible, in most areas, to reclassify many minor roads as bridle paths whilst maintaining motor access to the one or two properties along such routes. Equally, the use of powered vehicles (the notorious off-road driving) in open country, unless essential for land-management purposes, should be totally unnecessary.

The Ministry of Defence (MoD) use a number of our designated areas, for example in Dartmoor, the Brecon Beacons, and Warcop in the North Pennines AONB, for military training. They still use some of the designated areas for more than their fair share of the national need for low-flying training. That these special areas, land which we went to war to defend and protect as special quiet countryside should be so degraded by MoD generated noise appears a fundamental contradiction, even a defacement of their war memorials. The Countryside Commission recognised the need for a tougher stance against military training in National Parks *'The Commission understands, however, that new weapons and training needs may lead to demands for increased military areas in National Parks. The Commission will resist such demands, military training should take place in less sensitive areas outside National Parks.'* (Countryside Commission, 1985) The Commission achieved little in seeking to reduce the discordant military use of Dartmoor or the Brecon Beacons National Parks.

Figure 15: Pen-y-Fan and Cribin, Brecon Beacons National Park

Tourism is a curious word within a National Park context. It is used both in the sense of facilitating the enjoyment of the designated areas by providing accommodation necessary for visitors, but equally is an industry that takes on a life of its own. It can too often disregard the value of the setting in which it is based and see further developments as conducive to benefit tourism. It ignored what a planning inspector in the Lake District once cautioned – National Parks are not tourist resorts. The fear of such 'Blackpool' style approaches was uppermost in the minds of the fathers of the National Parks. Equally, if National Parks are to quote The Council for National Parks, the "test-beds of sustainable development," how then do we view the role of a tourist industry that relies, for the most part, on further use of the private motor car within the designated landscapes? How do we view the developments of 'wet-weather' facilities in areas famed for their outdoors, or conference facilities where delegates are virtual prisoners in airless rooms? Meanwhile the growth and expansion of caravan and lodge sites gradually eats into the fabric of the designated landscape, and the hotels seek the quality end of the market, thereby restricting the availability of accommodation for those least able to afford high costs.

Tourism in National Parks is too often devoid of the real National Park experiences, where visitors should have the chance to reflect and understand the landscapes, which surround them. Jim Crumley trenchantly argues *'National Parks have failed the landscapes of England and Wales by their inability either to embody the original long-lost ideals in enforceable legislation, or to stem the flood of visitor pressure which years of relentless promotion and self-flattery have generated.'* (Crumley, 1991) People should enjoy the quality of the character of the area gained, to an extent, from simply being quiet in that landscape rather than be seen as "milch cows" by a too often over-exploitive industry. Even that most timid of government agencies, the then Countryside Commission notes, recognising the appropriate place of the tourist industry in the economic well-being of National Parks *'excessive or inappropriate provision for tourism must be resisted.'* (Countryside Commission, 1985) Yet planners and the planning system are weak in the face of such onslaughts. Each National Park has its horrors of inappropriate tourism development, not least a significant number of large, intrusive or badly screened car parks, intrusive and mechanical or technological recreation, time-share or lodge accommodation, and conference facilities. Crumley, when he refers to the Countryside Commission for Scotland and local authorities, complains:

> *'The Lakeland experience has shown them that a defiled, exploited landscape is no deterrent to a certain strain of tourism, and all they would have to lose by so exploiting the Cairngorms is their credibility in the international conservation community, already aghast at Scotland's lack of commitment to its best and wildest landscape.'* (Crumley, 1991)

Perhaps the recent case (2013), debated nationally, about a proposal for a zip-wire in the Lake District fells reflects this is a continuing issue.

The use of National Parks by visitors for traditional National Park purposes is not without negative effect. Over-use of some areas is very serious – can you find peace and quiet on the summits of Snowdon, Helvellyn, Pen-y-Fan on most days of reasonable weather? Can you walk on some of the fells without adding to footpath erosion, sometimes exacerbated by bicycles or off-road driving? Such concerns are not new, as Nan Fairbrother expressed when she comments on the reports leading to the establishment of National Parks:

> *'Yet these early reports foresaw very clearly the difficulties ahead: If the Parks... will lead to the most serious*

consequences – in damage to amenities, in overloading and dislocation of transport, accommodation, and other facilities, in objections by the resident population and in initial discredit to the National Parks administration' The trouble has already started in the Lake District and Snowdonia, small and beautiful areas, long popular, and now within perilously easy reach of large urban congregations.' (Fairbrother, 1970)

Yet the ways we encourage the large-scale invasions, now in all seasons, affect the landscape, as it gains no respite from intensive use. The large-scale charity walks can quickly deplete a valleys water supply or clog up the local access or litter the area – as they frequently manage over several months each year in Snowdonia and the Lake District. Crumley summarises the problem *'Of course there is room for all, but only if we are to preside over the execution of the landscape – death by unnatural causes.'* (Crumley, 1991)

Since Dower various reports into National Parks have suggested that the second statutory purpose should enshrine their appropriate **quiet enjoyment;** enjoyment that was regarded as most fulfilling and having the least impairment of the beauties of the areas and of the quietude of others. Without such a change there will be an increasing conflict between the different users of the area who all claim their recreation comes within this purpose, a debate most significantly expressed during the inquiry into the Windermere 10 m.p.h byelaw.

Yet there is a need for visitors to spend their money wisely and ensure that local services are maintained and that locally grown products are consumed. When national chains, the ilk of Tesco, Costa Coffee, the Hilton hotels, establish themselves in the designated areas, they simply bleed a greater proportion of money spent in designated areas. This is money that should be vital to sustain a rural economy, and is transferred to other areas where there is already relative richness. The impact occurs through the import the raw materials of their trade rather than purchase the local lamb or traditional products that can better ensure the well-being of local communities. Expansion of such businesses, as with many tourism businesses, lead to low-waged employment, and more significant pressures on the housing system, largely through the need to import labour as it is not locally available. We need a basic reassessment if our designated landscapes are to continue to accept change and largely change which is detrimental to the future sustainability of those areas.

There are other aspects of our inadequate planning system to consider, in the sense of protecting our National Parks and areas of outstanding natural beauty, from major developments just outside their boundaries. This debate has been intense in recent years, as proposals to site major wind-turbine development have been considered. These are especially on sites just outside the boundaries of designated areas, so affecting the enjoyment of the landscape within these areas. Often the areas under consideration for the wind-powered power stations are in attractive uplands and sometimes reflect that the designation of our finest landscapes was based more on the pre-1974 political boundaries than on the quality of those landscapes. Hobhouse recommends the need to protect the settings of National Parks *'...from incongruous and unsightly development.'* (Hobhouse, 1947) We have few safeguards in place to achieve this aim.

Figure 16: Stanton, Gloucestershire within the Cotswolds AONB

Alongside the unfinished business of ensuring the designated area boundaries are appropriate in meeting the statutory purposes for designation, we still have areas lacking appropriate protection through designation. The northern Howgills, as an example, although the matter is now for consideration with the Secretary of State, fits within the need to extend the Yorkshire Dales National Park boundary. Equally the Cambrian Mountains should be the next National Park in Wales. The North Pennines, Nidderdale, and Forest of Bowland areas of outstanding natural beauty meet both statutory purposes for National Park designation and the Westmorland Fells between Tebay, Orton and Kirkby Stephen are more than meriting and in need of at least AONB protection and are regarded as being of National Park qualities. These later areas will face a public inquiry, in 2013, to examine if they can become part of the Yorkshire Dales National Park. All the potential and existing designated areas are worthy of a buffer zone in which major developments should only be permitted with an outstanding national need for such a sensitive siting.

Figure 17: The River Tees below Cronkley Scar, the North Pennines AONB. A potential National Park?

It is doubtful if designated areas can succeed with the delivery of their statutory purposes given the high levels of parochialism built in to National Park authorities. Their inability to consider their deliberations within the national status of their areas is legendary. But this was foreseen, as we have noted in chapter 2, by Hobhouse who recommends National Parks should be subject to a central planning authority. The seminal Dower Report assumed National Parks should be truly and fully national, provided for the nation and clearly provided by the nation. Such a body would need to be adequately funded and sufficiently independent, a role the forerunners of Natural England were ill-equipped to undertake. The same applies to Natural England itself. Haythornthwaite notes of the original National Parks Commission, the nominative national co-ordination and creation body for our designated landscapes, *'The embryonic Commission was divested of effective powers and robbed of its purse.'* (Haythornthwaite, 1960) from which the designated areas have never recovered. Most other countries, albeit of differing park types, have national units for running National Parks. A national service answerable to national politicians is, however, not what local politicians and some local residents' desire.

With some legally strengthened clarity, there are other tools that might be more effectively used. The Environment Act 1995 placed a statutory duty (s62) on government bodies and utilties to have due regard to the statutory purposes of National Parks. (For AONBs, there is a parallel s85 duty under the Countryside and Rights of Way Act 2000). Clarity to further this duty could bring about much needed relief on the pressures currently felt by the designated landscapes, more particularly if it were effected in a nationally co-ordinated manner. National Park Authorities have rarely exercised wisely or fully their enhancement of landscape statutory purpose although there are some good examples of small-scale landscape enhancements throughout England and Wales. Lack of funding and the complexity of funding streams is too often a hurdle. All government funding streams, be they for economic development, agricultural payments or lottery grants, should be handled directly by the designated areas. All land presently government and local government owned, could be passed into the inalienable stewardship of a National Park service. Encouragement should be given to landscape charities to own more land in such areas. Although there have been some significant examples of how not to manage such land by our most respected landscape charity, the National Trust, and on whose land and partially through its failure to ensure small farms are still extant, miles and miles of fencing littering the fells, and ancient semi-natural woodlands are managed for non-native species, are only a few examples. All such bodies should operate through established principles putting the national interest and reasons for designation as paramount considerations. Crumley believes *'The landscape must never again be treated as currency as it has been all too often for all too long. Heritage cannot be bought and sold – it can only be honoured or defiled.'* (Crumley, 1991) If land cannot be managed in such a way, it opens the door for a legitimate claim for it being nationalised. Hobhouse foresaw the gradual but inexorable acquisition of land for the nation as being desirable within National Parks yet some National Park authorities own little land whilst others are divesting their ownership to save expenditure. What more effective vision to realise for designated landscapes as Antoine de Saint- Euxpéry expresses well *'Our spiritual heritage must be preserved, else our people would be deprived of genius.'*? (de Saint-Euxpéry, 1942)

Many of the examples of how land might be protected for the future beauty and enjoyment of the designated areas were regarded as essential through the control of inappropriate activities. Ann and Malcolm MacEwen have provided a more closely argued appraisal of the ineffectiveness of those concerned with National Parks in meeting the ethos so well-articulated by the fathers of the National Park movement. Their 1987 book followed up with some more positive suggestions as how the National Parks might better respond to their challenges of that time. Whilst the development control process is seen as essentially negative, it has been shown where it has succeeded to be a most positive way of protecting cherished landscapes. (There are many cases where it has failed). It is easy to be critical of such processes but, given our recognition that conservation is the engine to manage the rate, scale and direction of changes, then the creative and constructive parts of the National Park movement has to demonstrate positive enhancements in the designated areas. The creation of new native woodlands in formerly wooded areas, the creation of wilder, more natural upland landscapes are but two of many challenges. The difficulty here may be in achieving this whilst keeping the cultural farmed landscape largely intact. There are many ways in which these areas can take a positive lead. This might be to show how the ethos of National Parks, notwithstanding the pressures for inappropriate change, is both as valid and important today as it was in the immediate aftermath of two world wars. Yet, whilst expectations of society are changing, the basic human needs are consistent and enduring. Designated landscapes need support and leadership to be both protective of the tradition of the endemic character of landscape, and able to meet the fundamental needs of humanity, whilst respecting the intrinsic beauty of place within the context of a changing society. Crumley analyses the problem for conservationists:

'For as long as conservationists are embattled and embittered by successive rearguard actions seeking to defeat or compromise the next development and the next, defending the landscape will be perceived by many people as a negative stance and a barrier to progress and prosperity. The landscape, meanwhile, is demeaned, locked into a spiral of decline by the perpetual quest for compromise.' He adds *'The launch of one sustained and supreme effort could prove to be a watershed beyond which the Cairngorms would be safeguarded as wilderness for all time and society would look at its wild landscapes with new and respectful eyes. Anything less clings to the futile status quo, and has damage limitation as its highest endeavour. The Cairngorms landscape deserves a higher purpose than that. It will be safe only when its protection is enshrined in law, only when legislation makes it unambiguously clear that the Cairngorms is not available for development, not available for poor land management, not available for thoughtless tourist promotion, not negotiable. Until then, the conflict created by compromise will be the principle arena into which energies are channelled, the landscape will continue to deteriorate; conservation will be condemned to a role of protesting villain and the tactic of rearguard action, and the public perception of a negative force; even development proposals which have been rejected, ..., can still be amended and resubmitted again and again if necessary, because the developers know that there is nothing in the planning system to stop it, and that sooner or later the opposition will weary as its resources dwindle and the public tires of its protest.'*
(Crumley, 1991)

Figure 18: Ramsey Island, Pembrokeshire Coast National Park

There is a wide acceptance of William Wordsworth's "a sort of national property' being the key phrase which led to the start of the National Park movement. For Wordsworth it was not just the phrase but the way he and fellow Romantics gave us all a way to view the countryside. The evolving movement was not to protect that landscape in aspic but to preserve the special qualities of the beauties of the countryside to raise the human spirit. The essence of the National Park vision was identified by Arthur Blenkinsopp as '*The National Parks stand for a scale of values that is in conflict with many of the pressures of our urban society.*' (Blenkinsopp, 1975). Therein lies the vision and the enigma we have to face today. So great are the battles, Wragg (Wragg, 2000) suggested, that because the continued attrition of rural landscapes is unrelenting it brings into question the protected areas approach of National Parks and areas of outstanding natural beauty. Paul Shepheard notes our current British landscape strategy is *'the economic exploitation of the earth"* from which we *"are simultaneously rewarded and deprived.'* (Shepheard, 1997)

It is now much more infrequent and more difficult under the pressures of modern life to equate beauty of landscape with human need, inspiration and aspiration. Landscape is too familiar in advertising but too rare in our considerations for equipping people to obtain a better quality of life. Landscape has become simply a backdrop, the scenery of commercial promotion of over-consumption. We do not sufficiently help new generations to understand landscape and its relevance to the quality of life in terms of an appropriate experience or of respect for the natural world we inherited. This is not to say we are all becoming philistines who abhor Nature. Alain de Botton expresses this dichotomy:

'Because we find places to be beautiful as immediately and as apparently spontaneously……it is hard to imagine there is anything we might do to alter or expand our attractions.' He continues *'We overlook certain places because nothing has ever prompted us to conceive of them as worthy of appreciation, or because some unfortunate but stray association has turned us against them.'* (de Botton, 2002)

It is simple and easy to apportion blame for the loss of the aesthetic appreciation of landscape on an increase in materialism. There is, additionally, the need to examine the introspection of the changing values espoused by those who are now charged with or find they are responsible for protecting our protected landscapes. The protectors predominantly take a defensive posture to protect the need to preserve in the face of a more demanding agenda from those who see economic progress as a single minded and dominant necessity. The result has been a breach of faith in the values of beauty that more urgently require the stoutest and most proactive defence. Harvey Taylor has other concerns:

'The obvious pertinence of ideas and issues ramifying from a late nineteenth-century concern with urban crisis and rural decline has resulted in often vaguely defined notions of an outdoor movement, which has been equated too readily with

those contemporary expressions of 'back to the land' philosophy which incorporates such progressive, planned, practical concepts as public parks, garden suburbs and garden cities. This misleading connection also places too much emphasis on the sort of nostalgic pastoralism that produced sentimental ossified reproductions of landscape, presented in late Victorian artefacts for the urban kitsch market, and generating a suburban villadom attachment to an idealised representation of southern English countryside.' (Taylor, 1997)

National Parks are far removed from this context; a recognition of traditional countryside character that defined and exhilarated the nation. They can still offer re-creation of the mind, body and spirit despite the exigencies of modern life. They are living, evolving landscapes that enable humankind to re-touch base; they are not for sale. Charlie Pye-Smith and Chris Hall recognise this problem as *'Symptomatic of our age are utilitarian values, and conservationists have been wary of expressing the moral, romantic and aesthetic reasons why they wish to conserve nature. Such timidity..., is stupid.'* They continue to remind us *'our ideals are fashioned out of a complex mix of emotion and desire, morals and ideology.'* (Pye-Smith & Hall, 1987) Yet we need to defend the moral and spiritual high ground of our arguments against the detractors of the National Parks.

Do we not owe to future generations a legacy of what is special and amply protected in order for them to seek the re-creation that gives the freedom to inspire creativity and to develop a relationship with their natural habitat? Surely, the development of a community and national identity along with a civilisation worthy of blossoming is a valued objective for our precious landscapes? To enjoy freedom and life we carry those concomitant responsibilities to society for the protection of landscape beauty.

The present and potential designated landscapes, our National Parks and areas of outstanding natural beauty, are frequently wilder places in the scheme of the English countryside. They also are places where people live and work but they contain glaring evidence of past and present abuse of those landscapes. Yet, they remain areas in which natural attributes can dominate and that can positively enhance the quality of human lives.

The pursuit of quiet enjoyment in these places is not elitist; they are available to all who would care to seek out their special qualities through stimulating their 'eye to perceive and heart to enjoy' as Wordsworth expressed. Whilst not all people can readily adopt those values, partly because they are excluded from appreciation of the countryside, that is no reason to compromise the intrinsic values of our dedicated landscapes. We have to work harder to achieve such progress, which Julian Huxley might have regarded as constituting *'the highest satisfaction...conceivable for men on earth...'* (Huxley, 1923)

There will always be people who find it difficult to feel comfortable when exposed to Nature. Paul Brooks writes:

'***What no floor show?*** *Fortunately the millions who visit the parks do not have identical objectives. There are some people whose physical metabolism requires an occasional dose of what Thoreau called 'the tonic of wilderness'. They are generally willing to work for what they get. Others go for fishing, for climbing, for photography, for nature study. Still others use the parks to give the whole family a week's inexpensive holiday in beautiful, healthy surroundings, they are probably happiest in a camp ground with close but congenial neighbours. ......All these concerns are equally legitimate. Unhappily, there is also a very different type of visitor – the type that comes looking for ready-made entertainment. He stops his car among the red-woods, rolls the window down for a closer look, and complains 'Yeah, I* *see 'em but what do you DO here?', as if he expected the forest to put on a floor show. He will certainly never find what he wants in the parks while they remain parks.'* (Brooks, 1976)

Paul Brooks' incongruent visitor is symptomatic of the current expectations of English society, as entertainment can only be meaningful if it has been directly charged to us, where quality equals high cost. The beauty of the countryside does not demand such immediate gratification as Pye-Smith & Hall recognise *'The benefit to society (of the countryside) should not be measured solely in pecuniary terms.'* (Pye-Smith & Hall, 1987) There is no need for the commercial spirit to supplant the needs of humanity. Nature is not for sale, so others steal it to the detriment of the landscape benefitting us all. These landscapes are unquantifiable and without monetary value. We must not defer to those who seek everything to have an economic value.

Many things have changed in society since 1949 as they have in the world of designated landscapes. In the latter, they are now overseen by a multi-functional organisation, Natural England, which has little power and little capacity to defend the interest of designated areas. We now understand more about the nature of landscapes and their value to people. The mapping of landscape character areas has provided a major step whereby local communities recognise what is special about their landscape as well as providing a useful tool for such activities as development control and assessing the nature and scale of landscape change. We are in a political time of limited resources and a government with less priority for protecting our National Parks. Originally, all-party consensus, in days after the Second World War, welcomed the 1949 Act. Today, the status of the National Parks is more politicised in parliament and yet their individual supporters are of all political hues. Perhaps because we have failed to make the National Parks into a national service, there are misguided questions about the National Park authorities, the nature of their governance and constitution particularly being viewed as undemocratic. We rarely make that accusation about other national services. In addition, this is in a time, when in all probability, the majority of residents of most of the original designated areas have freely chosen to live there since designation. We live in an age where we have more time for recreation, more need of that time and we have developed many new forms of recreation - mountain biking, hang-gliding, off-road driving, zip wires for example. Younger generations appear to need a more mechanical and technological aspect to their adventure and, without arguing against the validity of such activities, the question as to where is most suitable for these to be enjoyed is a highly controversial matter. We are now members of the European Union and the British government signed the European Landscape Charter in 2007. Additionally the nation was committed to ensure the conservation of biodiversity when it signed the Convention of Biological Diversity in 1994.

Some commentators regard the European Landscape Charter when coupled with the government's localism agenda, as potentially the end of any effectiveness by the managers of designated landscapes. All these changes raise questions of the fitness of purpose and the debates centre around the statutory purposes for these areas. These purposes not only encapsulate the values of the founders of the National Park movement but also should determine the foundation for actions, for government policies and funding, and they provide a test by which major planning issues should be determined. In addition, they underline the public reasons as why the areas are important and need public support as well as informing the international community that we do manage our cherished natural attributes to an appropriate standard. Any change to the National Park system would involve a statutory change to the purposes.

In 2010, the then chief executive of Natural England, Helen Phillips, suggested there should be a third statutory purpose, that of widening the recognition of the designated landscapes in ensuring we better protect our natural resources of air, water, soil, carbon sequestration, matters the current international agenda refer to as ecosystem services. (Phillips, 2010).

This matter and the review of the statutory purposes has been considered by Adrian Phillips for the Campaign for National Parks and his paper was discussed by their council in June 2010. This paper recognises the changes in legislative and international obligations since the statutory purposes have been before parliament, as well as many of the changes in the priorities of society. He suggested, as a first draft, that legislation might consider the National Parks having four statutory purposes. As CNP does not now cover areas of outstanding natural beauty no consideration was made as to which of his draft purposes might apply to these important areas.

Phillips' suggestions were:

'*1. To conserve and enhance the nature, landscape and cultural heritage of the area; 2. To promote public understanding and quiet enjoyment, including enjoyment of the special qualities of the area; 3. To maintain provisioning, regulating and supporting ecosystem services, including natural water storage, flood protection, and carbon sequestration and storage; 4. To promote sustainable forms of economic and community development which support the conservation and enhancement of nature, landscape and cultural heritage of the area.*' Phillips adds two important riders. The first *'if it appears that there is a conflict between any of the four park purposes, then greater weight must be given to the first of these purposes'* and '*public bodies should be required to further these purposes.*' (Phillips, 2010)

Figure 19: Staithes, North Yorkshire Moors National Park

The Sandford Principle, so called after one of the conclusions of the committee chaired by Lord Sandford to review the National Park system in 1974, is now enshrined in statute (following the Environment Act, 1995). In essence, this states that where there is an unmanageable conflict between the two statutory purposes of designation then the first conservation purpose takes precedence. Like many of the principles for our designated landscapes, the pre-1949 campaigners foreshadowed this.

Adrian Phillips recognises this principle and suggests it ought also to apply to his four suggested new statutory purposes. However, there is little to suggest this principle has been significantly prominent in the workings of some National Parks largely because of the politically over-bearing interest of economic development.

More pragmatically as regards the workings of the National Park authorities, but with one very significant exception, Phillips does not embrace in his paper the more common and often more frequently publicised and controversial issues of conflicts which arise within a purpose. Should, for example, there be priority for the promotion of agri-environment schemes which include a significant purpose of restoring upland flora, potentially at the expense of the cultural landscape of upland grazing on the commons? Should we enclose fell-side common land, even if only for a decade or two, to enable scrub woodland to develop even if there has been no evidence of trees in such locations for centuries? Should we allow for the low cost-benefit value policies for public goods resulting from significant payments to the agricultural community? Such are examples of current potential conflicts within the first statutory purpose in the upland National Parks.

Two nationally played out conflicts in the Lake District illustrate the tensions within the second purpose. In the 1990s there was the case made for a 10 m.p.h. Byelaw on Windermere with the implication of restricting fast power boating and water-skiing to the benefit of quieter, more active recreational use of the water. Despite a long running public inquiry and political interference, the decision was made to favour the more traditional uses of the lake. More recently, the application for a long zip-wire on Fleetwith Pike, above Honister Pass, raised similar issues. Phillips does suggest that the second purpose be amended to include the words "quiet enjoyment" which has been the objective of the founding fathers of the National Park movement, as with their successors, and would go a long way to resolving the issues inherent within the currently phrased second purpose. Behind such suggestions will be raised a fundamental question which is that of, for whom nationally are National Parks for?

Today we all too rarely hear the arguments for National Parks and for their value to society. Are we too arrogant to feel that such a case needs to be put, or do we feel that the war has been won and we can rest on our laurels? Can we regain the public support necessary to build on the vision of those who established the National Parks? Can we readily articulate the reasons why we need National Parks more today than ever before? Certainly, in the inter-war years we readily heard the case and the vision for the establishment of National Parks. Today we hear most about their problems and from their opponents. Richard Mabey notes *'We have been told their passion must be replaced by compromise and consensus.'* (Mabey, 1984) .You cannot compromise principles.

It is easy for the supporters of National Parks to point fingers at external threats to the designated landscapes. Before they do so perhaps, they should find a little time for introspection. Why has England so many conservation bodies? Some are small empires who have problems communicating with their supposed kindred bodies (even some of the larger bodies as the National Trust and the Royal Society for the Protection of Birds are not immune from such problems)? The split of landscape and nature conservation and the recreational lobbies, following World War Two, reflected government legislation in the National Parks Act of 1949, and enabled developers and government to divide and rule. The whole conservation movement lacks strength through fragmentation. To have a number of disparate organisations speaking on similar issues (for example, the Campaign for Rural England and the Campaign for National Parks) are expensive luxuries in the current days of cash-strapped charities. This is even more so when no government wants to speak to several bodies on similar issues. Then each National Park usually has a 'Friends of' organisation speaking locally but often unable to contribute at a national level. The local CPRE or National Park societies are often not aware of what their local Wildlife Trust or a similar body is saying or doing, and conflict of position is not unknown in the conservation world. If you read some press articles, for example in *British Wildlife,* you would think that the nature conservation lobby is at war with landscape conservation interests and especially so with recreational interests. Why have we missed the common purpose of the holistic value to humanity of the great British outdoors?

Add to this is the failure of many within the family of National Parks to explain the reason for their existence and, through their opposition to damaging schemes invoking the wrath sometime of local communities. This shows that any future strength of case involving ground-roots support needs to be clearly thought through and communicated to a wider public.

Even within National Park Authorities, there can be frissons, which undermine their very purpose. Rumours of the recently demised Regional Development Agencies softening up the development control mechanisms within parks is not new, nor is the claim that some senior National Park staff regard their statutory purposes as sufficiently unimportant compared with their perceived need to succour their critics in local communities. Some National Parks rarely consider their statutory purposes in arriving at development control decisions for major planning applications. If our National Park Authorities are not defending the primacy of our designated landscapes then who is?

If we can nurture, wisely steward, access and empathise with Nature throughout all of the wider countryside there should be no over-riding reason why we should forever retain the concept of designated landscapes. However, the key for now is enabling all our designated landscapes to enjoy an appropriate long-term symbiosis between the needs of people and of Nature, for they are frequently the last reserves of what we might lose or have already lost from the wider countryside. de Saint- Exupéry notes *'my civilization preached self-respect, which is to say respect for man present in oneself.'* (de Saint- Exupéry, 1942). We can show that respect through the way we respond to the landscapes we experience. de Saint-Exupéry counsels *'The important thing is to strive towards a goal which is not immediately visible. That goal is not the concern of the mind, but the spirit. The spirit knows how to love but is asleep.'* (de Saint-Euxpéry, 1942). Is it time for the spirit of landscape stewardship to be awoken? These are more than moral arguments, not just sentimental or impractical concerns, but the means to provide real human needs when they are urgently required. Can we look ahead with values intact and without the necessity of following transient fashions of modernity?

We have had National Parks for over sixty years and still too many residents, local authorities, governmental bodies, businesses and visitors do not know or do not want to know about the intrinsic value of these most special areas. Is it that National Parks have only been discovered by marketing people and by the tourist industry at large? The Countryside Commission believed if the National Parks *'are to remain as national assets then supporters for their objectives must emanate from the widest of sources.'* That mission has hardly yet been attempted and is sorely a necessity, urgently so. What the Countryside Commission noted over two decades ago is still urgent and our response lacks the urgency that is still necessary *'Changing patterns of agriculture and forestry, pressures for economic development, and an ever-increasing number of visitors erode the traditional character of the parks. Their beauty is fragile. All of us concerned about them must reaffirm the ideals for which they were created. We must consider how best we can secure their future.'* (Countryside Commission, 1985) That campaign quickly died after the National Park celebration ended at Chatsworth in that year, 1985.

People today do not know or accept the ideas of Wordsworth, Ruskin, Rosseau, they are no longer "cool", but does this invalidate their ideas and visions? Must we sweep away George Trevelyan's call *'The happiness and the soul's health of the whole people are at stake. The preservation of natural beauty as an element in our nation's life is a cause that deeply concerns people of every sort who are working to maintain any ideal standards and any healthy life.*' (Trevelyan, 1929)

Is it the time to develop a vision for the Parks for the future? Designated landscapes are not fantasies but are places of real values to the whole of our civilisation; they should be part of our staple diet which society in total cannot afford to go without. How they achieve such a value is in need of debate.

We have, to quote Ann and Malcolm MacEwen been *'going downhill'* ever since National Parks were created following the Act of Parliament in 1949 (MacEwen & MacEwen, 1982). Perhaps if we can rediscover the values underlying the original vision, values that would appear as appropriate today as in the decades leading up to 1949, then we may have the ability to re-promote and protect the values of our National Parks and turn the onslaught of those who see them as barriers to their personal economic interests. Perhaps, as Frank Fenner notes with respect to Nature, *'the primary need is a change in human values and our ideas of morality.'* (quoted in Passmore, 1974). In the end, it will come down to perceptions, understanding, commitments, and belief and how we can influence these for, as de Saint Euxpéry explains, *'to know is not to prove, not to explain. It is to accede to vision. But if we are to have vision, we must learn to participate in the object of the vision. The apprenticeship is hard.'* Hard it may well be, but let us hope it is not too late to undertake the journey for which Trevelyan bound us, to having vision and to keeping it alive for the future of humanity:

'Without vision our people will perish and without natural beauty the English will perish in the spiritual sense. In old days the English lived in the midst of nature, subject to its influence at every hour. Thus inspired our ancestors produced their great creations in religion, in song, and in the arts and crafts - common products of a whole people

spiritually alive. To-day most of us are banished to the cities, not without deleterious effects on imagination, inspiration, and creative power. But some still live in the country and some still come out on holidays to the country, to drink in with the zest of the thirsty man the delights of natural beauty, and return to the town re-invigorated in soul.' Later he adds *'If modern man needs to have his imagination kept in touch with the past and its spiritual and aesthetic values, even more does he require to be kept in touch with nature, as an offset to his imprisonment in the unnatural sights and sounds of city life. The effect of natural beauty on the mental and moral life of the individual is in the strict sense of the word "incalculable", but it is certainly immense.'*
(Trevelyan, 1929)

Figure 20: Warm Beck Gill, Roeburndale, Forest of Bowland AONB. An AONB with a greater proportion of access land than most National Parks

For Trevelyan, conservation and preservation was strong enough as an ethos for the welfare of human beings alone. If you add our increasingly valid awareness of the human responsibility for protecting wildlife and natural beauty for its own intrinsic values then the case for designated landscapes becomes invaluable and overwhelming.

BIBLIOGRAPHY OF SOURCES

Books

Appleton, J. (1990) *The Symbolism of Landscape*, Washington: University of Washington.

Appleton, J. (1996) *The Experience of Landscape*, Chichester: Wiley.

Ashby, E. (1978) *Reconciling Man with the Environment,* Oxford: OUP.

Baille Scott, M.H. (1906) *Houses and Gardens*, London: Woodbridge. (1995 edition used)

Bate, J. (1991) *Romantic Ecology – Wordsworth and the Environmental Tradition*, London: Routledge.

Batsford, H. (1946) *How to See the Country*, London: Batsford.

Brodie, I. (2012) *Thirlmere and the Birth of Landscape Conservation,* Carlisle: Bookcase.

Bronowski, J. (1973) *The Ascent of Man*, London, B.B.C.

Caldwell, L.K. (1972) *In Defense of Earth*, Indiana: Indiana University Press.

Camus, A. (1942) *The Myth of Sysiphus*, London: Hamish Hamilton, 1955 edition used.

Camus, A. (1947) *The Plague*, Harmondsworth: Penguin, 1960 edition used.

Camus, A. (1951) *The Rebel*, Harmondsworth: Penguin, 1962 edition used.

Camus, A. (1962) *Carnets 1935 to 1942,* London: Hamish Hamilton, 1963 edition used.

Camus, A. (1964) *Carnets 1942 to 1951*, London: Hamish Hamilton, 1966 edition used.

Cherry, G.E. (1975) *Peacetime History, Environmental Planning, Volume II: National Parks and Recreation in the Countryside*, London: HMSO.

Colegate, I. (2001) *Pelicans in the Wilderness*, London: Harper Collins.

Cornish, V. (1930) *National Parks and the Heritage of Scenery*, London: Sifton Praed.

Cornish, V. (1931) *The Poetic Impression of Natural Scenery*, London: Sifton Praed.

Cornish, V. (1935) *Scenery and the sense of Sight,* Cambridge: University Press.

Cornish, V. (1937a) *The Scenery of England*, London: MacLehose.

Cornish, V. (1937b) *The Preservation of Our Scenery*, Cambridge: University Press.

Cornish, V. (1943) *The Beauties of Scenery*, London: Muller.

Cousins, J. (2009) *Friends of the Lake District - the early years*, Lancaster: CNWRS.

Countryside Commission (1986) *The Lake District: A sort of national property*, Manchester: Countryside Commission & Victoria and Albert Museum (CCP 194).

Crowe, S. & Mitchell, M. (1988) *The Pattern of Landscape*, Chichester: Packard.

Crumley, J. (1991) *A High and Lonely Place,* London: Jonathan Cape.

Darby, W. J. (2000) *Landscape and Identity*, Oxford & New York: Berg.

de Botton, A. (2002) *The Art of Travel*, London: Hamish Hamilton.

de Saint-Euxpéry, A. (1939) *Wind, Sand and Stars*, Harmondsworth: Penguin, 1966 edition used.

de Saint-Euxpéry, A. (1942) *Flight to Arras,* Harmondsworth: Penguin, 1961 edition used.

Dubos, R. (1980) *The Wooing of Earth*, London: Athlone.

Edmonds, M. (2004) *The Langdales,* Stround: Tempus.

Fairbrother, N. (1970) *New Lives New Landscapes*, Harmondsworth: Penguin, 1977 edition used.

Gambles, R. (1997) *The Story of the Lakeland Dales*, Chichester: Phillimore.

Gardner, A. (1942) *Britain's Mountain Heritage and its Preservation as National Parks*, London: Batsford.

Hazlitt, W. (1822) *Selected Essays -On Going on a Journey*, Cambridge: University Press, 1924 edition used.

Hill, H. (1980) *Freedom to Roam*, Ashbourne: Moorland.

Huxley, J. (1923) *Essays of a Biologist*, Harmondsworth: Penguin, 1939 edition used.

Huxley, J. (1953) *Evolution in Action*, Harmondsworth: Pelican, 1963 edition used.

Irving, R.G. (1935) *The Romance of Mountaineering*, London, Dent.

Joad, C.E.M. (1928) *The Future of Life*, London: Putnam's.

Joad, C.E.M. (no date) *A Charter for Ramblers*, London: Hutchinson.

Joad, C.E.M. (1946) *The Untutored Townsman's Invasion of the Countryside*, London: Faber & Faber.

Kaplan, S. & Kaplan, R. (1982) *Cognition and the Environment*, New York: Praegar.

Keith, W.J. (1980) *The Poetry of Nature*, Toronto: University Press.

Koestler, A. (1978) *Janus*, London: Hutchinson.

Lowenthal, D. (1986) *The Past is a Foreign Country*, Cambridge: University Press.

MacEwen, A. & MacEwen, M. (1982) *National Parks: Conservation or Cosmetics?* London: Allen and Unwin.

MacEwen, A. & MacEwen, M. (1987) *Greenprints for the Countryside?* London: Allen and Unwin.

Macfarlane, R, (2003) *Mountains of the Mind*, London: Granta.

Mann, T. (1955) *The Confessions of Felix Krull, Confidence Man*, New York: Signet, 1963 edition used.

Meade, C. (1954) *High Mountains*, London: Harvill.

Muir, J. (1911) *My First Summer in the Sierra*, Edinburgh: Canongate, 1996 edition used.

Muir, J. (1913) *My Boyhood and Youth*, Edinburgh: Canongate, 1996 edition used.

Muir, J. (1915) *Travels in Alaska*, Edinburgh: Canongate, 1996 edition used.

Muir, J. (1916) *A Thousand Mile walk to the Gulf*, Edinburgh: Canongate, 1996 edition used.

Nicholson, N. (1955) *The Lakers*, London: Hale.

Nicholson, N. (1963) *Portrait of the Lakes*, London: Hale.

Nicholson, N. (1969) *Greater Lakeland*, London: Hale.

Nicholson, N. (1994) *Collected Poems*, London: Faber & Faber.

Nietzsche, F. (1889) *Twilight of the Gods*, Harmondsworth: Penguin 1968 edition used.

Nietzsche, F. (1892) *Thus Spoke Zarathustra*, Harmondsworth: Penguin 1961 edition used.

Passmore, J. (1974) *Man's Responsibility for Nature*, London: Duckworth.

Perrin, J. (2002) *Travels with the Flea*, Glasgow: The Inpinn.

Pye-Smith, C. & Hall, C. (1987) *The Countryside We Want*, Bideford: Green Books.

Rebuffat, G. (1962) *Between Heaven and Earth*, London: Vane, 1965 edition used.

Sartre, J-P. (1938) *Nausea*, Harmondsworth: Penguin, 1965 edition used.

Sartre, J-P. (1946) *Existentialism and Humanism*, London: Methuen, 1948 edition used.

Schama, S. (1995) *Landscape and Memory*, London: Harper Collins.

Shepheard, P. (1997) *The Cultivated Wilderness, or What is Landscape?* Chicago & Cambridge Massachusetts:Graham Foundation & MIT Press.

Shipton, E. (1936) *Nanda Devi,* London: Hodder and Stoughton, 1939 edition used.

Shipton, E. (1944) *Upon that Mountain*, London: Hodder and Stoughton.

Shoard, M. (1987) *This Land is Our Land,* London: Paladin.

Shoard, M. (1999) *A Right to Roam*, Oxford: University Press.

Smythe, F.S. (1935) *The Spirit of the Hills,* London: Hodder and Stoughton, 1946 edition used.

Smythe, F. S. (1941) *The Mountain Vision*, London: Hodder and Stoughton.

Solnit, R. (2001) *Wanderlust A History of Walking*, London: Verso.

Spencer Chapman, F. (1938) *Lhasa: The Holy City*, London: Chatto and Windus.

Stephenson, T. (1989) *Forbidden Land*, Manchester: University Press.

Taylor, H. (1997) *A Claim on the Countryside*, Keele: University Press.

Taylor, P. (2005) *Beyond Conservation*, London: Earthscan.

Thody, P. (1961) *Albert Camus 1913 –1960*, London: Hamish Hamilton.

Thomas, K. (1983) *Man and the Natural World*, London: Allen Lane.

Thoreau, H.D. (1854) *Walden*, Oxford, University Press, 1997 edition used.

Thubron, C. (1968) *The Hills of Adonis*, Harmondsworth, Penguin, 1987 edition used.

Wilberforce, W. (1779) *Journey to the Lake District from Cambridge*, Stocksfield, Oriel Press, 1983 edition used.

Winter, J. (1999) *Secure from Rash Assault*, California, University Press.

Wordsworth, W. (1805) *The Prelude*, Oxford, University Press, 1960 edition used.

Wordsworth, W. (1810) *Guide to the Lake District,* Oxford, University Press, 1926 print of the 1835 fifth edition used.

Wyatt, J. (1991) *The Bliss of Solitude*, Maryport, Ellenbank.

Wympher, E. (1871) *Scrambles Amongst the Alps*, London, Murray, 1985 edition used.

Edited Volumes of Chapters

Blenkinsopp, A. (1975) in *The Countryman,* August 1975 Issue.

Brooks, P. (1976) article in Atlantic Monthly as reprinted in Wildlife Review (a quarterly magazine 'Dedicated to the understanding and wise use of British Columbia's wildlife and other resources'. Autumn issue.

Holt, A. (ed.) (1985) *Making Tracks*, London, Ramblers' Association.

Horder, Lord (1937) in Williams-Ellis, C. (ed.) *Britain and the Beast*, London, Dent.

Howard, Lord (1937) in Williams-Ellis, C. (ed.) *Britain and the Beast*, London, Dent.

Joad, C.E.M. (1937) in Williams-Ellis, C. (ed.) *Britain and the Beast*, London, Dent.

Joad, C.E.M. (1944) *The Countrygoer* -Issue 1, 1944.

Mabey, R. (ed.) (1984) *Second Nature*, London, Cape.

McNeish, C. (2000) *Escape to the Hills*, Scottish Wildland News, Spring issue.

Mitchell, E.V. (ed.) (1935) *The Pleasures of Walking*, New York, Vanguard, 1975 edition used.

Moore, C. (1944) In *The Countrygoer*, Issue 1, 1944.

Serres, M. (2004) article in *Naturopa 102/2004*, Strasburg, Council of Europe.

Spence, K. (1937) in Williams-Ellis, C. (ed.) *Britain and the Beast*, London, Dent.

Stapledon, R.G. (1937) in Williams-Ellis, C. (ed.) *Britain and the Beast*, London, Dent.

Williams-Ellis, C. (ed.) (1937) *Britain and the Beast*, London, Dent.

Government Reports and Acts of Parliament

Abercrombie, P. & Kelly (1932) *Cumbria Regional Planning Scheme*, Liverpool: University Press & London, Hodder and Stoughton.

Addison Committee (1931) *Report of the National Parks Committee*, London, HMSO Cmd. 2928.

Dower, J. (1945) *National Parks in England and Wales*, London, HMSO Cmd. 6628.

Environment Act, 1985.

Hansard (1878) columns 1524-5.

Hansard (1946) 10 April 1946.

Hansard (1949) 31 March 1949.

Hobhouse Committee (1947) *National Parks (England and Wales) The Report of the Hobhouse Committee*, London, HMSO Cmd. 7121.

National Parks and Access to the Countryside Act, 1949.

Mattocks R H (1930) *The Lake District (South) Regional Planning Scheme*, Kendal, Atkinson & Pollitt.

Scott Report (1942) *Report of the Committee on Land Utilisation in Rural Areas*, London: HMSO Cmd. 6378.

Tracts

Anon (no date) *National Parks - An appeal to ramblers, cyclists, campers, hostellers, and all who love the beauty of Britain*, London: an amalgam of recreational bodies.
Countryside Commission (1985) *Watch over the National Parks*, Cheltenham, Countryside Commission (CCP 198).

Friends of the Lake District (1937) *Make the Lake District a National Park*, Ambleside, FLD.

Friends of the Lake District (1947) *National Parks –Their Purpose and Administration*, Ambleside, FLD.

Friends of the Lake District (1948) *National Parks or Local Authority Parks*, Ulverston: FLD.

Haythornthwaite, G.G. (1960) *The National Park Dilemma*, St. Albans, Youth Hostels Association.

James, E. (1928) *Safeguarding Lakeland*, Whitehaven, Whitehaven News.

Joint Committee for the Peak District National Park (1944) *The Peak District – A National Park*, Sheffield: JCPD.

Sayer, S. (1970) *Wild Country*, Dartmoor, Dartmoor Preservation Association, 2000 edition used.

Sheffield Campaign for Access to Moorland (2005) *Right to Roam*, Sheffield, Northern Creative Print Solutions.

Standing Committee for National Parks (1944) *National Parks*, London, SCNP.

Standing Committee for National Parks (1938) *The Future of National Parks and the Countryside*, London, SCNP.

Thirlmere Defence Association (1877) *The Manchester and Thirlmere Scheme - An appeal to the public and facts of the case,* Windermere, Thirlmere Defence Association.

Trevelyan, G.M. (1929) *Must England's Beauty Perish? A plea on behalf of the National Trust,* London, Faber & Gwyer.

Conference Reports and Proceedings

Appleton, J. (ed.) (1980) *The Aesthetics of Landscape*, Didcot, The Landscape Research Group and Rural Planning Services.

CPRE (1937) *Monthly and Conference Report, November 1937*, London, CPRE.

Federation of Manchester Ramblers' (1923 - 1939) *The Rambler's Handbook*, Manchester, Manchester Ramblers' Federation, 17 editions between 1923 to 1939.

Holmes, A. (1930) *The Ramblers' Handbook,* Manchester Ramblers' Federation.

Phillips, A. (1985) *The Consciousness of Landscape – The Making of the National Parks of England and Wales*, London, Victoria and Albert Museum (Typecast of lecture).

Phillips, A. (2010) *The purposes of National Parks - time to revisit the issue*, London: Campaign for National Parks Discussion Paper, June 2010.

Phillips, H. (2010) *Speaking Notes to the March 2010 meeting of the Campaign for National Parks,* Sheffield, Natural England.

Purves, L. (2000) *Internal Report to the Council for National Parks, June 2000,* London, CNP.

Trevelyan, G.M. (1931) *The Call and Claims of Natural Beauty,* The Rickman Gidlee Lecture, London, London University College and University College Hospital.

Journal Papers

Brotherton, I. (1985) Landscape Research, *Landscape Research*, **10** (1).

Sandbach, F.R. (1978) The early campaign for a National Park in the Lake District, *I.B.G Transactions and papers*, **3** (4).

Selman, P. & Swanwick, C. (2010) On the Meaning of Natural Beauty in Landscape Legislation, *Landscape Research*, **33** (1), pp 3-26.

Sheail, J. (1995) John Dower, National Park, and town and country planning in Britain, *Planning Perspective*, **10**.

Wragg, A. (2000) Towards Sustainable Landscape Planning: Experiences for the Wye Valley Area of Outstanding Natural Beauty, *Landscape Research*, **25** (2), pp. 183-200.

Documents

CCC County Archive Service, Carlisle file DSO24/9/1

Friends of the Lake District - various internal files.

Himsworth, K. (no date) personal communication of notes of speech, *National Parks - In the Beginning.*

Stephenson, T. (1969) *The Campaign for Countryside Legislation 1929 - 1968,* London, Ramblers' Association, September 1969 - an internal typescript.

www.ingramcontent.com/pod-product-compliance
Ingram Content Group UK Ltd.
Pitfield, Milton Keynes, MK11 3LW, UK
UKHW041942190726
13854UKWH00004B/1744